QUEERSTORIES

QUEERSTORIES

EDITED BY MAEVE MARSDEN

hachette
AUSTRALIA

hachette AUSTRALIA

Published in Australia and New Zealand in 2018
by Hachette Australia
(an imprint of Hachette Australia Pty Limited)
Level 17, 207 Kent Street, Sydney NSW 2000
www.hachette.com.au

10 9 8 7 6 5 4 3 2 1

Introduction and selection © Maeve Marsden 2018

NATIONAL
LIBRARY
OF AUSTRALIA

A catalogue record for this
book is available from the
National Library of Australia

ISBN: 978 0 7336 4072 8 (paperback)

Cover design by Grace West
Cover photographs courtesy of Shutterstock and Stocksy
Text design by Bookhouse, Sydney
Typeset in 12.5/18.6 pt Adobe Garamond Pro by Bookhouse, Sydney
Printed and bound in Great Britain by Clays Ltd, Elcograf S.p.A.

MIX
Paper from
responsible sources
FSC
www.fsc.org   FSC® C001695

The paper this book is printed on is certified against the
Forest Stewardship Council® Standards. McPherson's Printing
Group holds FSC® chain of custody certification SA-COC-005379.
FSC® promotes environmentally responsible, socially beneficial
and economically viable management of the world's forests.

CONTENTS

INTRODUCTION

Queer spaces have always been hidden: down a back alley, behind the bushes, a secret handshake. Our community is as much defined by our codes and furtive glances as we are by our flagrant, garish pride parades. In the past we may have been hiding from the law, but even now queer spaces are little refuges from a world that may delight in gay narratives about family acceptance and marriage, but will shy away from our dirty sex or complicated relationship structures. From the thud and grind of a dancefloor, to the reflected light of inner city beats, we make these places to find each other and to feel at home in a society that defines gender as a binary, and sex as biology, that likes our rainbow flags and covets our culture, but still wants to limit our access to power; our ability to transform the world not just ourselves.

Queerstories, an LGBTQIA+ storytelling event that I host and program, began as part of the City of Sydney's Late Night Library program in 2015 at Kings Cross Library in the heart of Sydney's historically gay district. I was inspired by the library – a place of stories and history, an intersection of public and private lives – to create an evening of queer storytelling, a platform for the stories we don't always hear in the mainstream. 'Don't tell your coming out story or give a speech about same-sex marriage,' I told the storytellers. 'Tell the story you share when you aren't performing for the straight gaze.'

And so, from there, Queerstories grew. In a time dominated by debate over the legalities of our lives, Queerstories became a space for subtlety and complexity, allowing us to celebrate our community through storytelling, rather than political campaigning, opinion pieces and speeches. And still the stories were inherently political, because it remains a radical notion to prioritise the marginalised and outsiders over the status quo.

For the last two years, Queerstories has found its home in Sydney, where each month I program six storytellers, asking them to tell a ten-minute tale from their lives. I choose a combination of those who already have a public platform, as well as those who don't. The stories are shared on a podcast and now, as word has spread, I've been able to expand the event, travelling to other cities and towns. Queerstories' premise isn't inherently revolutionary or original, its popularity merely relies on our community's need to carve out space for ourselves, come together and build connections.

For me – a child raised by lesbian mothers, now a queer woman myself – producing and hosting Queerstories has been a homecoming and, as an artist and producer, it is the project that most reflects and celebrates my identity and community. The faces may have changed from my early childhood, but that room full of LGBTQIA+ people is every 'Lesbian Mothers with Children Group' meet-up at a community hall in the 90s. It's the Judy Small concerts where she sang about feminism and union rights, and Chris Miller translated her words into Auslan side of stage. It's every protest march, though with less chanting, and every Mardi Gras, with less nudity.

Collected in this volume are 25 of my favourite stories from a diverse pool of storytellers who have performed at Queerstories in Sydney, Melbourne and Brisbane, as well as a story of my own. Traversing decades, these pieces capture what I love about our irreverent and irrepressible community. I am honoured to share them with you.

JOHN

Jen Cloher

Nineteen eighty-six in Adelaide was all about *Whispering Jack*, Lady Diana blow-waves and Kylie's debut on *Neighbours*. The end of each working day was punctuated by Dexter running stats on a couple's compatibility as Greg Evans leapt around the stage in Hush Puppies. Paul Hogan's *Crocodile Dundee* took the world by storm, while the lesser-known masterpiece *Malcolm* caught the attention of more discerning moviegoers.

I was twelve and looked like a boy. So much so that I got looks when I walked into the ladies' toilets at the Hoyts cinema. I owned a silver BMX with blue tyres that my parents had embarrassingly assembled for my recent birthday. When not at school I wore black ripple soles, Levi's, a black Bonds T-shirt and a Ford jacket. Holden jackets were not cool.

In 1986 I lived my life outside of my Catholic Girls' School largely as a boy. I also had a dirty secret. I was addicted to

Galaga, the Namco video game sequel to 1979's Galaxian. The game play of Galaga puts you in control of a spacecraft situated at the bottom of the screen, with enemy aliens arriving in formation at the beginning of each stage trying either to destroy, collide with or capture your spaceship. The player progresses every time alien forces are vanquished. Galaga is one of the most successful titles from the golden age of arcade games – Pac-Man, Ms. Pac-Man and Donkey Kong. I knew a good game when I played one.

The closest Galaga tabletop was about 2 kilometres from my house in a corner store next to St Peter's Anglican Boys' College. This is where the sons of wealthy Adelaide radio personalities were schooled and where whole tribes of South Australian farming offspring were sent to board. The classic St Peter's casual attire consisted of a pair of R.M. Williams boots, beige work jeans, blue and white striped shirt (sleeves rolled, collar up), and a Driza-Bone.

I was schooled at the Catholic ladies' equivalent, Loreto College. Iron-fistedly ruled by a coven of Irish nuns, we were tortured daily with thwacks to the back of our legs with a wooden ruler. Adelaide is famous for its churches and murders and one can quickly see how they came to live side by side.

The life of a boarder at a religious school seemed like a sad one to me. Each Friday as other kids looked forward to weekends in the surf or speed skating at Downtown, boarders had to go back to the same four walls. The corner store was a nearby outlet for boredom and I'm pretty sure the St Peter's boarders kept their business afloat. My dedication to Galaga was so great that I was prepared to sit and play on a Saturday afternoon surrounded by a pack of St Peter's brutes. My expertise soon grabbed the attention of a few regular gamesters and before long I was drawing a crowd as I furiously jerked the joystick back and forth, annihilating one row of alien bees after another.

One day, a large thuggish redhead with a litany of freckles called Davo asked me what my name was. This was no place for girls. 'John,' I replied, holding my breath while I waited to see if he bought my disguise. Davo looked at me for a few seconds and then said, 'John does alright for a little fella.'

And so I became John, the little guy on the silver BMX with blue tyres, purple reflector sunglasses and a Ford jacket. Months passed and my status as an expert grew. Now, when I walked into the store I was greeted with nods of recognition. As I sat down with my Farmers Union Iced Coffee and a neat stack of twenty-cent pieces, a crowd would form to see if I could top my previous high score.

Life as John was comfortable. At Loreto, I was confused daily by the endless rules and protocol of being a young lady. Young ladies cross their legs, don't shout, pull their socks up, wear stockings in winter, wear a blazer when travelling outside of the school grounds, never open their mouths when masticating food, never talk unless they are spoken to, wouldn't be seen dead on a BMX. The rules were endless and dull. They meant nothing to me. I lived for the weekends when I could transform once again into that confident, sexy little man in black: John Cloher.

Keeping up a habit is expensive. To fuel my weekend binge I needed at least ten dollars. This was stolen from my mother's coat pockets, my father's bedside drawer and a collection of books in the study where my parents stashed their bigger notes. It started with some small change, a handful of fifty-cent coins and the occasional two-dollar note, but soon I was snatching purples and blues from the pages of *Pride and Prejudice* and *Gardening Australia*.

Thankfully my parents were busy people and my long absences went largely unnoticed. I would rise early on a Saturday morning and pedal down to the only 24-hour McDonald's in Adelaide. As I scoffed down my cheeseburger, I could feel the butterflies in my stomach. Soon I'd be at the corner store, playing Galaga. There was nothing in my life so performative, adrenalin-filled and thrilling. Nowhere that I felt so adequate and successful. It was in this tiny corner, surrounded by St Peter's boys, that I was liberated. Where I could truly be me. Where I could live freely as John.

All deception runs its course and my halcyon days were numbered. One learns in life that everything passes, both the good and the bad. My schoolwork was suffering and I was deeply unhappy at Loreto. I had friends at school, but most of them were fast becoming girls. Ra-ra skirts and bubble dresses were the latest fashion craze as Madonna and Cyndi Lauper topped the charts. I was also starting to discover that no matter how hard I tried I couldn't get a boner for Christian Corveaux. Sorry, Christian, if you're out there and you've got your hands on this book, because somehow you ended up being a gaylord too . . . You were no doubt adorable, but no matter how many times we spoke on the phone after school, I just didn't feel that special thing.

I was neither a girl nor a boy. I was just me. No matter where I looked I couldn't find a place to belong. I didn't even know what a lesbian was. The word 'queer' was used to describe dirty old men who hid in parks waiting for children to walk past. A positive non-binary experience growing up wasn't a reality back then. Adelaide in the 1980s was not a place where you discovered gender as a journey rather than a destination. It was a place you survived.

The character I identified with most was E.T. I even dressed up as E.T. one Halloween. I was into outsider role models, you see. And just like E.T., I was somehow trying to phone home. Planet Earth made no sense to me. There must be somewhere out there where little people like me could just be . . . left alone.

End of term was fast approaching and I had an essay due on Monday. My mother, Dorothy, a tall, proud and brilliant academic, had confined me to my room to study in preparation. As I sat poring over my history books I could feel the first thought drop in, a warm explosion in my stomach. I longed for the feeling that came with completing level 10, just before the first 'challenging' stage, with a double fighter ready to obliterate a swarm of alien wasps. That sense of achievement as '10 000 points PERFECT score' flashed across the screen with a triumphant bleat from Galaga's catchy theme song.

I could take it no more. I threw down my pen and moved quickly and stealthily to the study to grab some cash. My mother was in there working. Never mind. Next, to my Dad's dresser drawer. Empty! Just a few days prior, Lucy Turnbull had stopped past, collecting for her MS Readathon. In a rare and desperate move I went direct to my mother's purse. It was slim pickings: a fifty and a twenty. Whatever I took would be noticed but I no longer cared. I placed the twenty deep in my back pocket and mounted my silver steed.

Like most Saturday afternoons, the shop was pumping. The smell of Balfours pies and pasties heating in the warmer, a fresh batch of Allen's Strawberries & Cream on the counter, and, as I sat down, the faint smell of cigarette smoke on some of the older boys. I had now earned such a reputation that I was given the table as soon as the game was over. Taking my seat, I felt the adrenalin catch up with me. There'd be some explaining to do when I got home, but for now I was safe. I took a big bite of my Crunchie and settled in for the long game.

Things were off to a good start. Having passed the first two challenging stages with a perfect score I was two men up and armed with a double fighter. I sailed through Level 30, where most players become unstuck as the speed of the game increases. Another challenging stage and a perfect score. I had now clocked 250 000 points and had a serious edge of about twenty people around the table trying to catch a glimpse of what was coming next. Even Mick the shop owner was watching. After Level 40 he gave me a free bottle of coke. I took a massive gulp before firing into the next round.

I was now at the eighth bonus stage and about to clock close to half a million points. My highest score ever. Each time I completed a stage a cheer would resound, my pals slapping me on the back with approval. I was in new territory, levels none of us had ever seen before. It was thrilling. As the next stage began, Davo leaned close to my ear: 'Go, John. You got this, mate.'

It was then that I started to notice a commotion near the door, where out of my peripheral vision I could see a tall shadow had appeared. I looked up to see, to my horror, my mother standing there. I looked down, hoping somehow that the crowd would conceal me. But it was too late.

'Jennifer, come home at once!'

Silence. Followed by the loud explosion of my fighter blowing up. And then it slowly dawned on the boys who Jennifer was. I sat there like a lump. 'At once!' my mother barked.

I stood up and started to walk towards the door. A couple of the boys sniggered, but the general mood was one of shock. John was Jennifer?! My face crumpled as I slowly climbed into our baby-poo-coloured Volvo, overcome by feelings of shame and defeat. My cover blown, I never went back to the store again.

Jen Cloher

Jen Cloher is an ARIA nominated artist who has released four albums. Her most recent, self-titled *Jen Cloher* (2017), is the culmination of a period of artistic and personal growth in which she took her rightful place as the punk-rock figurehead of Melbourne's famous DIY music scene.

A NIDA Graduate, Jen is an outspoken advocate for artist rights and the co-founder of the incredible Milk! Records label that she runs with Courtney Barnett. In 2011 Jen launched a series of workshops called I Manage My Music, specifically tailored to assist the self-managed musician.

COUNTRY SPEAKS TO US
A MEANDERING FISHING YARN

Steven Lindsay Ross

I am literally the worst fisherman ever.

I always suspected that I was a flawed Aborigine. I used to love wrapping a long white towel around my head to pretend I was Agnetha from ABBA, or dancing around the clothesline to Amii Stewart's 'Knock on Wood'. I wasn't sure how that equated to being less Black but to some boys and men in my family, being 'girly' was definitely not Black.

Others just noticed the difference without judgement, like Aunty Lois, who, when discussing Mardi Gras with Aunty Pam, would say, 'They're really creative, those sexual people, aren't they, not like those non-sexual people?'

Kuka Laura riled against that typecasting, though.

In 2008, some twenty-four years after she passed into the Yemerreki (Dreaming), I thought of her. It was one of those dusty, oppressive, hot days in southern New South Wales, where a cold beer tastes like the best thing in the world and where buzzy clinging flies become body accessories. I was trying to slip a slippery river shrimp onto my hook, a process I never loved, in between big swigs of ale that barely touched the sides. I hooked my finger instead, in a flurry of swearing, sweat and blood. I pictured Kuka and a few other ancestors shame jobbed with their faces in their palms.

Kuka Laura, my grandmother, was a crack fisherwoman. Actually, in my mind she was a superhero. A hunting, fishing, animal-skinning, mussel-diving, wild Salvation Army tambourine-swinging, one-eyed Wonder Woman, who brought up all of her nine children, a bunch of rogue kids, a few grand-children and a yard full of animals.

Like all good superheroes, she lost her eye in a chemical accident during an experiment with oven cleaning that went wrong. The loss of her left eye never impinged on her ability to accurately hurl an object at a lippy grandchild or, in a flash, grab a scurrying child who cheekily poked his finger up the arse of a very clenched and pinched Pentecostal minister.

Kuka was a woman of few words, even if you count speaking in tongues. The most she spoke was during the Bible study sessions she ran for the grandchildren around the church's hexagonal white laminated table on a Saturday afternoon, preparing us for the doomsaying on the Sunday. The other times she spoke a lot was ordering us around before an impending visit from white people – what we called 'a welfare visit'. Our housing commission house in Ballantyne Crescent, Deniliquin, would be sparkling, its laminex surfaces scrubbed and its linoleum floors hosed out.

To admit to being a bad fisherman is not easy for a proud Wamba Wamba man. Fortunately for me, nowadays I can go to my local supermarket for a slab of salmon rather than relying on my catch of the day. Kuka Laura did not have that luxury in our small town, equipped only with a sparsely stocked Millers Supermarket and a couple of butchers selling only marbled, fatty lamb and beef.

Kuka was always supplementing our sugary, flour-coated Western diet with native foods. One day, she'd serve up freshly caught kangaroo or that honorary bush food, rabbit; another she was diving for mussels in the Koletch or fossicking for mushrooms in a muddy paddock. And of course she would take us to her favourite fishing spots, particularly near the bridge that crossed the river near Moonahcullah, the former mission.

Koletch – a river white people call 'Edward' – meanders out of the Murray River near Mathoura in southern New South Wales and grinds westerly through Barapa Barapa and Wamba Wamba Country, converging with the Wakool River after being fed by countless creeks, runners and little watercourses. It passes through the bustling little towns of Deniliquin, Wakool, Moulamein and Tooleybuc, and re-enters the Murray at Kyalite.

Koletch was the original riverine course of Mile, or the Murray River, until a massive earthquake thrust some 20000 years ago changed it to its current course.

Kuka Laura, a Mutthi Mutthi woman, married my Ngupa Neil, a Wamba Wamba man. He also loved fishing but it was mostly her domain. I remember her taking us to dive for *pithen* (mussels) and netting *lip-lip-wil* (yabbies) in the shallow sandy parts of Koletch. We were in awe of this voluminous woman – normally so staid and mostly sedentary – moving through the then clear water with grace and dexterity, gathering up mussels with a swish of her hands, collecting them in the lap of her house dress. We giggled with the wonderment of all kids who see their parents or grandparents do something adults just don't do. We were thrilled.

My mate and cousin George told me a yarn about this place on the Koletch called 'the Bulger' – this deep hole below the brown and swirling water that Kuka would deep dive into and come up with her shirt bulging with *pithen* and *lip-lip-wil* . . . hence the name 'the Bulger'.

Kuka tried to teach me to fish despite my revulsion for impaling worms and ripping open shrimp. In later years, I would try to employ these skills fishing with my sister and her partner at the time, but I rarely succeeded. It would be normal for the two women to be pulling in *pangal* (Murray cod) either side of me and for me to be reeling in twigs, plastic bags, the occasional muddy shoe, more often than not getting fucking snagged on submarine tree roots. That is my lot in life: to be surrounded by great fishers.

Ironically and cruelly my totem is the *kurng-kurng*, or kookaburra, a magnificent kingfisher.

Totemic identity is one layer of identity for Aboriginal people. Add in tribal or national identity, cross-tribal identity, kinship connection, specific geographic part of country, matrilineal or patrilineal, language groupings – things get complicated.

It is part of the supposed contested identities of being Aboriginal in contemporary Australia – as a great friend of mine Anita Heiss once wrote, 'Am I Black enough for you?' Mind you, the only people to seriously attempt to make me feel less Black are white people, with questions like 'What percentage are you?' or 'You're not full-blood, surely?' I have never been quite sure how to answer this, except to state, 'I am Wamba Wamba.'

As a young and impressible man-child at Sydney University in the 1990s, I was, for a short time, inevitably recruited into and inculcated by a young socialist club. I was hypnotised by hot, young, disillusioned men in black, who mesmerised me with phrases like 'cognitive dissonance' while gulping cans of Coca-Cola. I remember the moment the socialist romance abruptly ended.

After being swept up in a beat-up old Mazda from my parent's house I was spirited away to a meeting in Marrickville. After a few mind-numbing hours of proletariat preaching we emerged in a trance and crammed into an old banged-up Holden with several other people, exhausted from feigning interest with the requisite repetitious knowing head nod.

The only other Koori in the group began testifying to the virtues of a worker's interpretation of the universe while sucking on cigarette after cigarette. He stated with authority that to truly understand the workers' struggle I had to relinquish my

Aboriginality – my family, kinship connections, land, water, spirit, ancestors – everything that I knew and sustained me.

Everything that sustained a people for 60 000 years. So young, I hadn't even held down a job yet. I had no idea about the workers' struggle. The choice was easy.

These are the kinds of false choices required of Aboriginal people in Australia. People often try to force you into their tribes, their boxes, their identities. Sometimes you're forced to see identity as layers or priorities, a false hierarchy created without consent. Being Black and gay creates even more complexity.

I like to think of identity as resonating from a person, like light, rather than being created in sedimentary layers. That light is made of a spectrum – many parts that make up the whole. This metaphor would work more fully for me if light wasn't white, but I think you get my point.

The tension created by contested identities becomes tough when you're out, because the gay community is just as racist or ignorant as the general community. I remember my lovely ex-boyfriend telling me snippets of what white gay men say about Black gay men in all-white company: 'Aboriginal men are so secretive,' they say. Maybe we're just sick of constantly explaining ourselves, our families and our cultures to everyone; sick of being objects of curiosity when we interact with non-Aboriginal people.

You don't have to explain your relationship with your Kuka. Most people know that special connection with a grandparent, the connection of blood and love, of country and knowledge. This person made possible your present, but they have experienced a time and place you never will.

My sister Laura and I spent a lot of time with Kuka Laura during our childhoods as our mother Jeanette worked a lot, including regularly looking for work in Sydney. In 1982, Mum went to France for three months and Laura and I were sent to Deniliquin for the whole year – hardly second prize, but it was when I spent a lot of time with Kuka Laura. This time is precious to me now, since she died two years later, in her early 50s.

Kuka used to let me stay up late to watch old movies with her, or Wimbledon. I think she knew I was unusually interested in Stefan Edberg's legs. I am grateful that in all of time and history, of the thousands of generations of Aboriginal people who lived in Australia, I got to spend those precious moments with her. Someday those moments will be forgotten and fade from humanity and the life of the Earth, the Sun and the Milky Way, but just for the moment we had that.

Unfortunately, I also witnessed her blood lust for killing innocent bait to nefariously feed to other animals on a metal instrument of death. I saw her snatching them in their sucking lip or mouth, then violently pulling them, gasping and flailing for liquid oxygen, into the vastness of our poisoned atmosphere, where she'd promptly knock them on the head, rip their scales off, gut them from stem to stern and delightedly consume them.

She taught me to skin and gut kangaroo and rabbits. I was the only kid who was made to do this onerous task and I resented it. In hindsight, it was consistent with her desire to never box me in. She made me feel worthy to receive cultural knowledge as one of the tribe, part of an ancient unbroken line of Wamba Wamba people.

Although Kuka Laura was a good, God-fearing Christian, I don't think her lessons were intended to prepare me for the impending doom of Judgement Day. It is, however, comforting to know that when the apocalypse comes and the skill to gut and skin a kangaroo is required, I'm your man.

One hot and dry summer's day in 2008 I decided to spend time in the bush with George, another proud Wamba Wamba gay man, who helped me navigate coming out as a teenager, helped me find a way to live openly in a town of just 8000 people.

Like Kuka, George was a gun fisherman, reeling in everything that had gills and fins, in complete contrast to my inanimate object angling.

We drove his jeep deep into Werai Forest – the world's oldest river red gum forest of some 16 000 hectares, replete with wetlands, creeks and ceremonial burial sites there since the dawn of time. The name Werai, like everything about modern Australia, is a corruption word, formed from a farming acronym: 'We are A-Grade 1', a type of license for sheep droving. Our name for Werai is Pengalite, meaning a gathering of many clever men or witch-doctors. *Pengal* also means Murray cod.

This is the forest that sheltered the local Wamba Wamba and Barapa Barapa peoples from the onslaught of colonisation. In the 1840s, some eighty survivors of that violent and jolting process walked out of Pengalite. Every single local traditional owner owes their life to those brave eighty souls, and to the forest. There are thousands of us now.

George and I arrived at a spot called the Bunyip Hole, a well-known deadly fishing hole. I thought my fisherman moment might have arrived, but I soon discovered that my 'reverse magic' was contagious. Nothing was biting, moving or rippling the surface of the slow-moving and rolling brown water – not for me, and not for George.

I suggested that we cruise over to another part of the forest near Colligen Creek, a place where the local traditional owners camped and fished for thousands of years. We were joined there by Sharnie, my sister's girlfriend at the time (and our cousin – very distant). We walked to a serene little spot on the low bank of the creek where a bed of *wangel* (cumbungi reeds) and logs apparently created the perfect hiding place for fish.

As I was about to cast in a line a sudden wind blew up from the south. We turned our eyes skywards as a dusty *ngarak* (whirl-wind) rustled and violently tugged at the branches of trees that looked down at us from the high bank. We have always deified *ngaraks* – they are how clevermen travelled across and through Country. This particular mystical transport danced through several trees and, to our astonishment, twirled down the high bank onto the water, where it skimmed, shimmied and skipped across the creek, making it gurgle and splash.

The *ngarak* then leapt onto our bank and continued its dance deep into the forest, shaking and rustling river red gums in his wake. We were stunned.

Sharnie, who had always been windy and superstitious, screamed that we should get out of there. But I said, 'Fuck it, I'm throwing a line in', and I whirled my shiny sinew with its tasty payload into the spot near where the *ngarak* had pierced the water. It landed with a satisfying plonk.

No more than ten seconds later, just as I settled in, expecting my usual disappointment, I felt a powerful and unfamiliar tug on the line. Aghast, I reeled in a fucking whopper of a Murray cod. For the first time in my life.

In that ancient forest of clevermen and witchdoctors I like to think that that *ngarak* was sent by my Kuka, dancing through the forest to drop off a little gift and to remind me of her omnipotence; of the omnipotence of all my ancestors.

Ecstatic and wanting to bask in my fishing expertise I quickly drove home to my mother's farm. Her farm, which my parents bought in 2000, stands some 15 kilometres from the mission where she ran around as a little girl; in 1968, the entire population of families were forcibly relocated into Deniliquin.

I've got to say the reactions from my proud Mutthi Mutthi *kuyinggurrin* (mother) and my stepfather threw me for a six.

When I relayed the story to Mum she launched into a rather bland scientific explanation of how the whirlwind dropped red dust onto the surface of the water, ionising it, and that the agitation of the creek piqued the attention of the cod.

My white stepfather, on the other hand, said in a hushed tone, 'Oh, that's a sign.'

Whether thanks to science or signs, the fish was delicious and sweet and didn't last long.

Country speaks to all Aboriginal people, whatever our layers – or spectrum – of identities, whether we are straight, gay, Muslim, Christian, a parliamentarian, a lawyer or a buttoned-down public servant like me. That connection to Country is not easily severed – not by invasion, colonialisation or attempts at assimilation. That day and every day Country speaks to me, George and Sharnie and thousands of other Black gay, lesbian, bisexual, transgendered, intersex queers.

Country, like my magnificent Kuka, informs and drives our lives at a deeply profound level, inextricably and often intangibly. She may make a kingfisher out of me yet.

Steven Lindsay Ross

Steven Lindsay Ross is a Wamba Wamba man from Deniliquin in southern NSW and has cultural and familial connections to the Wiradjuri, Mutthi Mutthi and Gunditjmara peoples. Throughout his life, Steven has been a dancer, singer, actor and storyteller, and has designed and delivered cultural events and cultural education projects.

Steven has worked in the public service in Indigenous policy, environmental affairs, LGBTQIA+ projects, cultural and arts coordination, and local government. Steven has sat on the board for Murray Catchment Management Authority, Yarkuwa Indigenous Knowledge Centre and South-West Regional Arts. He is currently a board director for Inner City Legal Centre and Moogahlin Performing Arts, and sits on the Advisory body for the NSW State Library.

PASSING TIME IN WEST BERLIN
Simon Hunt

On the 1986 summer's day they excavated the Gestapo torture cells, I felt I was losing my sense of time. Late at night, three drunken friends and I climbed under the police tape and down into the pit of damp, recently-turned earth, whispering as we explored the too-small, white-tiled rooms filled with scattered debris, entombed since the final 1945 bombings. Mud-caked clipboard folders, broken shelves – even a wartime calendar that seemed like a film prop.

I picked up a small glass ampoule and held it up to the moonlight, imagining an SS officer drawing out its contents with a syringe, about to extract information from a prisoner in unspeakable pain. I saw this scene in scratchy, black-and-white 16 millimetre film, because that was the media distance that had cushioned World War II into a seeming fiction throughout childhood. But here, now, time is falling apart – the earth smells fresh, the glass ampoule is clear – perhaps I'm the first person here since the final bombardment, was it just yesterday? But then time flips the other way and I'm in the ruins of Pompeii, trying to extract meaning from the debris of a distant culture, lost in an antiquity that returns me to the comfortable remove of cinematic fiction.

Paradoxically, I'd felt that I was in a futuristic sci-fi movie when I arrived in West Berlin a few months before with my band, four days after the Chernobyl disaster. The Soviets were still underplaying it, but high radiation readings on food trucks arriving via East Berlin told the real story. On the first day we were told not to eat any fresh fruit or vegetables, the city living on a diet of meat and canned food for the next few months, café tables with abandoned salad left on the plates.

As storm clouds drifted across from the East on day two, the American Forces Network radio interspersed its regular badly acted, 1950s-style 'Watch out for spies!' commercials with advice to keep out of the rain, because it might be radioactive. Ignoring this advice, we head for the 1936 Olympic stadium in battering rain, manned with industrial-sized umbrellas; at the age of twenty-four, you're going to live forever, and there's so much to do in a new town.

We're the only people at Hitler's grandiose stadium, and in the thunderstorm we stand in our umbrella circle around the giant Olympic bell. Its raised swastikas have been clumsily welded over, then scratched back in again, scratched out, scratched in.

West Berlin was to have been the first stopover for my band before moving to London, but we quickly fell in love with this quirky, contradictory outpost of the Great Western Way, ringed in on all sides by the collapsing economy of East Germany, and inhabited by anarchist artists who responded to the constant physical reminders of the Cold War with creative reinterpretation and exuberant graffiti. A train line a block away from my house ended abruptly at the Wall, upon which artists would rotate murals of sunsets, train disasters, wartime scenes. Utopia, dystopia, utopia, dystopia.

The bizarre separation of the city quickly became normalised in my daily life. I would sunbake naked on the Kreuzberg riverbank with Dean, our other keyboard player, right next to the Wall. Officially, the narrow bank was East German territory, even though physically on the Western side. One day some guards leaned over the top of the Wall, telling us that we were trespassing on East German land. As we realised that they were not allowed to come over, we'd just laugh them off. Twice a week, an American tank would suddenly roll into the suburban street, a gunner with dark sunglasses sitting at the top. The American and Russian soldiers would photograph each other across the Wall for five minutes, and then the tank would roll back around the corner. I never worked out exactly where it came from.

Every day I'd catch a train from home to my band's rehearsal studios. Both of these places were in West Berlin, but due to the oddities of the Wall, the train line passed through old, crumbling East Berlin 'ghost stations', unused since the city was divided in 1961. Although these underground stations had identical architecture to the Western stations, they were blocked off to the public, lit only by a few flickering fluorescent tubes, and always guarded by two East German guards with guns. The trains would pass through slowly and not stop until we reached the next Western station. It was astounding to see the first few times, then it gradually became subsumed into your consciousness, and you'd keep reading your newspaper.

Today, I'm watching Stephen on the train as he experiences it for the first time. A friend-of-a-friend from Sydney, he's on a European arts junket. He's carting around a collection of Australian Super 8 films between different experimental festivals, and is always on the lookout for a party. His peroxided blonde hair is brushed up stiffly on all sides, and the flash of the passing fluorescent tubes across his hair gives him the look of a cartoon character in constant surprise.

Earlier in the day, I'd asked him to help me carry bags of coal to my apartment, so that it would be warm for the evening. '*So* medieval!' he exclaimed in his sardonic-Sydney-queen tone, a sound I found alien after a year in Berlin, yet still comfortably familiar. I like him, I decide, even as he struggles with the bag up the five flights of stairs.

In the afternoon we attend his Super 8 screening at a small cinema, with the requisite ten people who always attend experimental film festivals. Many of the Australian films seem to consist of European films that have been filmed off television, then re-edited with added drone soundtracks. They seem strange to watch here in a European cinema.

'Can we go to some East Berlin gay bars?' he asks, and I realise that I don't even know if such things exists. My world is a predominantly straight electronic music scene full of people who take more drugs than me. I occasionally furtively dart into nights of disappointment at local Western gay bars, but I soon leave, irritated by the music, and not confident enough to sustain conversations or make friends. I want gay friends, but I never seem to have anything in common with them, just quick sex and then I'm gone. I doubt things will be any better on the eastern side, but a few phone calls later, we've got an address so I'm about to find out.

The train emerges from the darkness of the ghost stations to East Berlin's Friedrichstrasse, which functions as both line exchange and border crossing. Long, winding queues to reach the glass window where you hand over your passport, and then you get the famous East Berlin triple scan: the official stares at you for five seconds, stares at your photo for five seconds, then cycles this two more times. With German body language, the length of time that you're socially allowed to stare at someone is much longer than in Australia, and in my first few months I misinterpret curious stares on public transport as a desire to either fuck me or kill me. East German border guy is clearly in the killer category. Nevertheless, with a grunt and a jerk of the thumb we're ushered into East Berlin on a day pass.

Late-1987 East Berlin looks like a 1950s Western city, but there's a transition over the first block where you pass through a few tawdry shops directed at Western tourists. The record shop consists of several racks of four approved records, themselves encapsulating the journey back through the decades: Michael Jackson's *Thriller*; Pink Floyd's *Dark Side of the Moon*; Carole

King's *Tapestry*; and The Beatles' *Revolver* – all actually new releases due to recent Soviet cultural relaxations under Mikhail Gorbachev.

At the end of the street, peeling paint and buildings still riddled with wartime bullet holes announce the end of the transition to the East, and as evening falls we follow the map a few blocks to our scribbled address. All eyes pivot to Stephen and me as we walk into the bar, and we quickly embark on a walk of shame to a spare booth. It's like a narrow fifties-style milk bar: long rows of small booths, mirrors on both sides, and superfluously overdecorated with multicoloured lamps of all shapes and sizes, all dimmed low. Some of them are on small shelves; others are roughly taped to the mirrors, as if a terrified lamp shop owner had desperately tried to get everything off the ground before a flood. Generic jazz wafts from a scratchy record, topped by a chorus of whispers from individual booths. There's no general interaction, with individuals walking back and forth to the service area to whisper their orders.

Where are we? Is this even a gay bar? We're about twenty years younger than everyone here, and heads spin around in booths as if sensing us from behind. I walk over to the bar and spend half of our money on two beers; the East German government slugs you so hard with the exchange rate when you cross back to the West that it's not worth trying to exit with any change. When I get back to the booth, a man with an exuberant, theatrical comb-over is trying it on with Stephen, and their lack of common language is resulting in nothing but embarrassed smiles. 'I need to film this place,' says Stephen, after the man fades back into a distant booth.

Just as we're discussing our escape plan, a young guy leans his back against the drinks area, and faces the booths with a studied nonchalance. James Dean, but with a broader forehead, an unnecessary scarf and a fake leather jacket that would cower in surprise if ever connected with a motorbike. A few dim figures immediately pop up from the booths and walk over to him, negotiating in low tones, before the victor marches him out the front door. Grim.

Five minutes later we're outside again, trying to work out the next step. Should we cut our losses and return to the hi-NRG disco palaces across the border? A guy who's sitting on a low wall asks me for a cigarette, and we get into conversation. He doesn't speak English, so I occasionally translate for Stephen. Klaus is an eighteen-year-old local meeting friends at an 'underground party' nearby, and invites us to join him. Stephen wants me to ask him about gay bars, but I sense that Klaus is straight, and I don't want to risk any homophobia before we've had a chance to check him out more.

We set off, and 'nearby' turns out to be a half-hour walk. Street lighting becomes sparse as we move further from the centre, and I start getting a little worried about the midnight deadline for westerners to be back at the border – often a drunken, jovial sprint that belies the serious consequences of breaking any rules in this country. I've got more questions for Klaus than he's got for me. Although he's never seen the other side of the Wall that's fast receding in the distance, he's happy enough with the general impressions he's picked up from his dad's secret TV in the attic, illegally scanning the American Forces Network and the West German ZDF. The West is nothing more than an idea, and he's cottoned on to the way that West Germany pumps money into West Berlin in order to present the visual contrast with the poorer, unconstructed East.

Finally we reach the warehouse. Stephen and I exchange grins as Klaus literally does the secret knock and gives the secret password, 'Kultur' (culture). It takes a moment for my eyes to adjust to the dim lighting, red-and-blue cellophane covers draped over rows of light bulbs. The last chorus of the Sex Pistol's punk anthem 'Pretty Vacant' is blasting through the small distorted PA system, and about twenty teenagers pogo up and down on the dancefloor. They're wearing classic 1976 punk gear – ripped tartan, leather, torn T-shirts and piercings that I quickly deduce to be artificial. It's like a shot from a TV commercial for *20 Greatest Punk Hits*.

Just as we sit down, the music abruptly switches to 1950s rock 'n' roll. The punks sit down and are replaced by young couples dressed immaculately for the occasion – full poodle skirts, greased and coiffed hair, practiced dance routines. They shake, they rattle, they roll. As my eyes adjust, I see that everyone's aged about sixteen to eighteen – we've ended up at an 'underground' Saturday evening school dance. The music switches between punk and rock 'n' roll every three or four songs, yet there's a peaceful coexistence between the two halves of the crowd, who talk among themselves and wait patiently for their turn. Klaus, one of the oldest here and commanding some respect, leads us to a darker corner where vodka is quietly added to the cordial jars. Why is this being kept secret? Klaus says some of the kids here have informer parents, and that even though they're attending an illegal event, they might create chaos if they go home drunk. The underground party has its own underground.

The Russian vodka takes hold, and we relax into our unexpected evening. A girl called Beate tries to teach Stephen some basic German, which becomes a source of laughter for our corner group. Everyone's friendly; it's completely different to the gay bar. We talk a little politics, and I ask them if they like Russian leader Mikhail Gorbachev, who'd been loosening some controls in Russia. *'Gorbachev ist Spitze!'* ('Gorbachev is the best!'), says Klaus, 'but he won't do anything for us here.' I tell them how a few months ago we'd all gone to protest against Ronald Reagan's stagey appearance in front of the Brandenburg Gate, but the Berlin police had shut down public transport for two hours before the speech, leaving Reagan to shout, 'Tear down this wall!' in front of a handpicked group of sycophants. None of them even knew that Reagan had visited, so it seemed things had been shut down on both sides.

Klaus has just bought the four-years-late *Thriller* album, and tells me that next month he wants to play some MJ songs at the club. We laugh as we imagine the new third faction trying to fit in between the punks and rock 'n' rollers, and we start singing musical riffs from 'Wanna Be Startin' Somethin''.

Suddenly, overhead white lights blast on, and the music stops. I panic. Is this a raid? Only Stephen and I are reacting, so I ask

Beate what's going on. 'We're having a fifteen-minute break,' she says with a smile, wandering off to refill the cordial jars. 'What are we having a break from?' Stephen asks Klaus. 'From the atmosphere, of course.'

People wander around, visit the bathrooms to check their look, but don't seem to be leaving – and indeed, after fifteen minutes the overheads are switched off and the party immediately resumes. We later discover that official state-led youth dances have a compulsory fifteen-minute break, and that this practice has simply been carried through into illegal, underground dances.

We're completely smashed by the time we reach the border, ten minutes before the midnight deadline. The streets are quiet; most have bedded down for the night. Klaus points to the Wall. 'Look at that thing,' he says, and suddenly grabs me by the waist, lifting me up. 'When I was a kid, I wanted to see what was over it. And now . . . You know . . . sometimes I wonder if there's anything worth seeing there at all. Maybe not . . .' He trails off, not quite finishing his drunken thought. 'But that's just a place. The people are different. You people are *Spitze*!' He lifts me a little higher into the air before comically dropping me to the ground.

'*Schwule?* (Gay?)' he asks, pointing to Stephen and me. 'Yes,' I reply. 'I'm not!' he says. 'But we are all happy in the world together!' It's a Disney moment, but there's real heart in it, and we all embrace before Stephen and I head back into the station for the triple face scan, followed by the ghost station trip back to the West. Fluoro light flashes jolt us awake from our vodka-filled stupor. Stephen kisses me, but I gently pull back, holding his stare to an almost German length, smiling at him. I've finally made a gay friend, someone I hope I'll always know, and I don't want to ruin it.

Simon Hunt

Simon Hunt is a composer, performer, activist and writer who lectures in Media at the UNSW Faculty of Art & Design. He has won awards internationally as a film-maker and composer, and recently composed the soundtrack for William Yang's ABC documentary *Friends of Dorothy*.

Simon is best known for his character 'Pauline Pantsdown' – a drag simulacrum of politician Pauline Hanson – who enjoyed a top ten hit in the 1990s made from Hanson voice samples, and has more recently operated online as a virtual activist and satirist.

He tweets from **@PPantsdown**.

FOR I HAVE SINNED

Amy Coopes

I was very good at liturgical dance. My talents, in fact, extended to all things piously Catholic. I had an angelic singing voice, the crisply enunciated consonants of a June Dally-Watkins deportment school graduate, and a histrionic streak that would put Pontius Pilate to shame. A precociously literate autocrat, I ruled Sunday School with an iron fist, appointing myself narrator of the annual nativity play and pedantically correcting the teacher at every available opportunity on her grammar, spelling, and interpretation of the Good Book. At school, I triangulated the perfect vantage point from which to surveil the staffroom door on a Wednesday afternoon, when the altar boy and liturgical dance roster would be posted for the coming week. Speed walking down that corridor and seeing your name on the list was truly an ethereal experience for an A-type authoritarian extrovert like me.

While I was as accomplished at the trappings as the most devout of Trappists, the gospel truth of the matter was, I was not a very good Catholic. Part of the problem was that I thought too much. I overthought everything. If those melt-in-your-mouth wafers were the body of Christ, what about the packet mix cupcakes that had one on top? If the priest was working on Sunday, wasn't he committing a sin? If loaves and fishes were God's chosen Happy Meal for the masses, why weren't we allowed to eat a Filet-O-Fish on Good Friday? If the poor were blessed, why was the Church always asking us for money? For a religion named after a guy called Chris, we sure talked a lot about this Jesus bloke.

Punctiliousness was one thing, but the real issue lay with my moral compass, which was calibrated rather perpendicular to true north. The worst thing most seven-year-olds had done was lie to their parents about their homework, or preyed upon a shift-working parent to double dip on pocket money entitlements. Already a hardened criminal, I was running a black-market business in my Central West schoolyard with stock stolen from the storeroom of my parents' general store. I nicked toys and trinkets when the corrugated iron shed out back was left open on stocktake night, and sold them to classmates for tuckshop profit. It was a neat little business, keeping me in fish fingers, pizza pockets and pies, and ensuring a steady stream of play date invitations to some of the most exclusive addresses in Parkes.

It was a heady few months before an unfortunate raid on my bedroom cupboard and subsequent interrogation by the local police (my parents held the station sandwich contract) derailed my larcenous excesses. Chastised, and circumvented from further felony via a rather imposing deadlock, my last stand took place during the annual Book Week Parade. Employing an elaborate *Wizard of Oz* Tin Man ruse, I waited until we were on the main street to up-end a bucket over my head and cock my fingers into pistols, shouting 'Hands up, in the name of the Kelly Gang!' My eye holes were, unfortunately, rudimentary at best, and we had barely moved a block before I had veered, blinded by plastic, off the road entirely and into a bemused group of onlookers. Such is life.

Thus was my quandary, as the occasion of my First Confession drew near. For a young Catholic, there could be no more formidable occasion than this. Yet I was riven by indecision. Should I share the full extent of my delinquency, or just make something up? What if I told the priest the truth and he revoked my liturgical dance privileges, or kicked me out of Sunday School? Or worse, what if I came clean and he cursed someone to die for my sins? This was my best understanding of Jesus at the time: he was just in the wrong place at the wrong time when a wizard – possibly named Chris – got pissed.

The technicalities of Confession were ambiguous, and they kept me up at night for weeks. Did you have to confess your 'worst' sin, or would any old infraction do? And how much detail was required? As long as I declared I had stolen, did the volume or nature of the larceny matter, really? As far as I could tell, all was forgiven in the end – being Catholic was good like that. God absolved murderers, robbers, even babies! If he could excuse Ned Kelly, surely he'd go easy on a prepubescent gangster like me.

When my life of crime had eventually caught up with me, I did what I'd always done: blamed my brother. No matter the indiscretion, this was my default, and the more inconceivable it was, the more stridently did the lady protesteth. Cat thrown into the pool? It was my brother. Window broken? It was my brother. Hundreds of dollars' worth of stock vanished from the storeroom as, by freak coincidence, a tuckshop bar tab materialised at the Holy Family Primary School in the name of Amy C? There was only one culprit it could possibly be. An audacious play given that, when he was scapegoated for my plush toy racket, Tim was three. It was inevitable then that, as my First Confession loomed, I found a way to inculpate my brother, declaring before the entire congregation that while I had 'taken' a toy, it had only been from him. Two Hail Marys and I was home free.

My sacramental sacrilege didn't improve. I ripped my stockings after falling out of a tree at my First Communion and said the word 'shit', which was pretty much the worst transgression you could commit in front of my mother. This was unfortunate given she'd married a RAAF airman who had delighted in telling me years earlier that his natty little forage hat was called a 'cunt cap' and used to wake me up of a morning with the refrain 'Wakey, wakey, hands off snakey'. I was quite genuinely nineteen years old before I realised what this meant.

By sibling contrast, my brother was an angel. He didn't steal; he didn't lie. He didn't cheat or worship false idols; he honoured thy mother and thy father. Blessed is the meek, for he shall inherit the Earth. He was a good Catholic, in the actual sense that matters. But he was a terrible showman, and there wasn't a sacrament that he couldn't balls up.

For reasons no doubt mysterious, Tim had an anxious temperament. He was highly strung, prone to the vapours. He would vomit at the slightest provocation, and with great verve. Every Sunday after post-Mass yum cha we would be treated to a second coming; his pork bun resurrected, his dim sum come again. He hurled his way from Warner Bros. Movie World to the Great Barrier Reef, and chundered across the Bass Strait from Launceston to Lorne. The only thing consistently capable of calming his nerves was Doritos, a brackish talisman that occupied a good square metre of our pantry and on which, for all intents and purposes, he appeared to subsist.

When it came to initiating Tim into parish life, my parents were a little lax. They didn't get round to having him baptised until he was four, and instead of an heirloom lacy gown, he wore a tracksuit. By that time we were living in rural Tasmania, so warmth and comfort were at a premium. While the priest recited the fine print on eternal damnation, Tim entertained himself by sliding up and down the pews before, imprudently sticking his head through a gap in the seat. By some freak of physics, he couldn't pull himself free again, and the more frantically he tried, the more firmly he got wedged. It took divine intervention in the form of anointing oil and holy water to ease him loose, and for weeks he reeked of myrrh. And vomit.

The most legendary parable in the Coopes family canon, however, concerns Tim's First Confession. He's a man of few words, my brother, and still waters run deep. Growing up in a military household had impressed upon us both that there was only one good greater than God, and that was hierarchy. Where my difficulties with religion were primarily theological, Tim's hinged almost exclusively on a fear of authority. He fretted for weeks about talking to the priest; had we noted the steadily mounting pile of Dorito packets under his bed, we might have had a clue, but by that stage I had hit puberty and was far too busy penning anguished journal entries about the torture of my existence to notice his distress. In preparation for my Catholic Confirmation, I had chosen St Bernadette of Lourdes as my saint, and was very much taking her patronage of those ridiculed for their piety to heart. I may have been an eleven year old living in suburbia, but inside I was an urchin trapped in a French dungeon, gripped with feverish visions of the Immaculata.

The day of Tim's confession dawned like a Dorito – crisp, and replete with unblemished promise. School shirt ironed with defence force precision and a comb tucked into his sock elastic, he was ready to renounce sin and be faithful to the Gospel. His insistence that the back window be wound down and white-knuckled grip on the seatbelt as we hurtled towards the church should have set the sanctus bells ringing, but a resurrection of breakfast had necessitated some costume changes and we were pushing it for punctuality. By the time we parked and made it inside, the pews were packed and it was standing room only. I'll never forget Tim's peaky grimace as he was pried away from the loving bosom of his family and hauled up the front to sit with his classmates.

The service passed in a blur of remonstrations – fire this and brimstone that – as I scowled at the objects on the altar, willing them to levitate and afford me a fast track to canonisation. Forget virginal visions, Roald Dahl's *Matilda* was more St Amy of Strathfield's style. As the priest droned on, I mentally hoisted the chalice and ciborium, scattering their contents over the bowed heads of the congregation like fish and chip dregs flung with abandon into a stiff ocean breeze. I had spent so much time in a saintly strabismus of late that my parents had been summoned to the school to discuss the possibility that I needed glasses, and they had dutifully shipped me off to an optometrist who declared that I had 20:20 vision and probably had trouble catching thrown objects because I was 'slow'.

Eventually, it came time for the moment of truth. Biliously, Tim rose from the pew, shuffling like a death row inmate towards the ultimate penance. His comb bobbed, askance, from the brim of his sock, as his weedy little legs propelled him up the carpeted steps to the priest, who sat astride a plastic stool in benevolent repose. Trembling, he lowered himself into the opposing chair, blessing himself with a left-handed, anti-clockwise sign of the cross. At the Michael Jackson-obsessed age of six, he was still writing his name backwards – M-I-T – and seemed at times to dwell in a sinister mirror-image underworld where everyone did the moonwalk and eating was a reversible activity.

The priest leaned forward invitingly, the corners of his eyes crinkling in paternal reassurance. Every muscle in Tim's sinewy little body was tensed, the ruminant bulbs of his rabbity little front teeth forming a bulge beneath his cats-bum-pursed lips.

Frowning, Father repeated his overture, charitably concluding that the organ's reedy squall had drowned out his initial request. Come on, the congregants seemed to urge, shifting ever so slightly to the edge of their seats. Dad was poised with his Pentax zoomed to its zenith over a sea of heads, the viewfinder fixed on the ashen pixels of my brother's panicked mug. Tim drew a billowing sail's worth of breath, staggered backwards from the priest, and pierced the close, perfumed air with a scream, bolting knobbled-knee over ankle down the aisle and out the narthex doors. Like a contagion, five other bug-eyed baby confidantes followed suit.

'Shit,' muttered my mother, hustling her way over laps and handbags to run after the shrieking gaggle, the Catholic families of Strathfield gaping in fascinated horror. Dad and I slinked out behind her, the organist valiantly playing on.

Head between his knees in a nearby gutter, Tim was hysterical, and no measure of cajoling or threat could convince him to re-enter the church and seal the sacramental deal. Defeated, my parents drove us home and prepared a panacean corn chip platter; a pagan Eucharist which, once served, freed my brother to confess. I was not permitted into the sanctum for this settling of the score, but the walloping I received shortly after did little to abate my Marian persecution complex.

According to my brother – in a ribald fiction I contest to this day – I am alleged to have told him that priests, like vampires, require certain sustenance to survive. Where Dracula lusted for blood, however, the frocked gentry (I claimed) were fuelled by sins. Confession was like bloodletting – a gory but necessary task for men of the cloth. Without it, I told the credulous younger Coopes, the priest's very life was at stake. Bearing in mind I had won actual awards at school for my 'vivid imagination', I had not – he swore – been content to leave it there. Oh no. Elaborating on my vision, I claimed that if you got to the altar and couldn't think of anything to tell the reverend his head would explode, like a malfunctioning android powered by infant shame.

Suffice to say, I was prohibited from speaking to my brother about religion after that, and the next year was blacklisted from attending his First Communion. Incensed, I attempted to have the sacrament annulled on the grounds that, given he had never completed his ceremonial confession, he wasn't eligible. Unfortunately, by that point my parents had sent him to a different school in a bid to rehabilitate his religious credentials, and the paper trail between the two parishes had run cold.

It was the beginning of the end of the road for the Catholic church and me, with the exception of a brief evangelical phase when I was fourteen and realised that Bible study was a byword for summer camp – a promised land of horseriding, swimming and sexual awakenings. It was here, at Teen Ranch, that I realised I was in love with my best friend, and that my stricken obsession with Gillian Anderson was textbook Same-Sex Files. Returning to school the next year, I refused to take the Eucharist, and was placed on a month of lunchtime detention in the chapel. Handed a toothbrush to clean the – mostly female – statues, I was encouraged to reflect upon the mysteries of God, and reflect I most certainly did. Cleanliness was indeed next to godliness, and the finer features of those women had never gleamed so white. Emboldened, I stepped up my campaign of passive resistance, continuing to eschew Communion and slipping further and further back through the pews until I was seated in the last row and could, when the nearest teacher bowed their head in supplication, slip out the back to the boarding school dining room for some actual bread.

I fell head over heels for a succession of women – teachers, older students, friends. At every turn I was silenced, and silenced myself. Someone dared to ask in a form meeting when we were sixteen which steps you were supposed to learn at Deb Ball practice if you were planning to bring a girl instead of a boy as your date. The teacher, who had all the hallmarks of a deeply depressed Catholic dyke, turned a particularly incriminating shade of vermilion and hissed that there were 'no girls like that at this school'. Eventually, I came out as gay, and vividly remember our first PE class thereafter, when another student complained to the staff that she didn't want me to be allowed to change with the rest of the girls any more because 'she'll try to look at us'. I was humiliated.

In that heady final HSC year of high school, when you felt on the precipice of literally anything, I had a torrid, tempestuous fling with a classmate, the kind where you took every opportunity to lay hands on one another and had each unpatrolled corner of the school committed to memory – equipment sheds, the music rooms and, yes, the choir loft. I have never felt closer to God than finding myself, sweaty and half undressed in the arms of another teenage girl, as a mass struck up in Latin below. *In excelsis Deo.*

Amy Coopes

Amy Coopes is a writer, journalist and doctor-in-training based in Albury, on the border of New South Wales and Victoria. The daughter of a RAAF medic and airman, she spent her childhood in a moving truck, changing schools with the seasons. There were only two constants in the chaos: Catholic school and writing.

After graduating from Charles Sturt University with a journalism degree and a student politician's knack for stirring trouble, Amy spent ten years as a news reporter, covering conflicts, coups and calamities, both in Australia and abroad as a foreign correspondent. An avid mountaineer and cyclist, Amy has a Masters in Writing and is also one of two mothers to a rambunctious young son.

THE EVERLASTING OPEN FAMILY

Paul van Reyk

My eldest daughter Mary got married five years ago. Not gay married, married married. My eldest son Rajendra got married last month. Also married married. To misquote dear old Lady Bracknell: 'For a pro-feminist, anti-patriarchal gay activist father to have one child marry may be regarded as a misfortune; to have two children marry looks like carelessness.'

How did I get to this sorry state?

I never expected or wanted to be a dad. Though I grew up in a Sri Lankan Burgher (mixed race) Catholic family, I can't recall ever feeling the weight of expectation that I would fulfil the Biblical imperative to 'Go forth and multiply'. Actually, there were no discussions about sex at all. When I was fifteen, my dad gave me a Catholic manual called *On Becoming a Man*, clearly hoping it would allow him to avoid having to have 'the talk' with me. I read up to where it started talking about masturbation being a sin that led to general moral and physical degeneration, and then I promptly abandoned my studies. I'd been jerking off pretty much every night since I was twelve. If the church wanted me to give it up, I would have to give up the church.

I had girlfriends during high school but they were good Catholic girls, so sloppy tongue kissing and the occasional grope of a fully-clothed tit in the back of my dad's car were as far as we ever got. Then I spent the first years of university stoned or tripping, so sex was the last thing on my mind. All through my mid-twenties I kept desperately falling in love with men. I'd get the odd fondle when they came home drunk and I was crashing on the bean bag in the lounge room of their share house, but I hadn't got around to being honest with myself about being gay yet. I'm still not sure what on earth I thought I was doing with these guys. I was still a virgin.

Then Dianne, a good friend from my uni days, returned from Europe, and within the course of a week I was no longer a virgin and had begun what became a six-month live-in hetero-sexual relationship. When it ended we stayed friends and she asked me to promise that if she ever wanted to have a child I would be the father. I agreed. I liked Dianne very much and didn't want her to be disappointed by a 'no'. Anyway, it sounded so far in the future as to be unlikely ever to happen.

A couple of years later she rang to take me up on my offer.

The timing of Dianne's request had the potential to be very awkward. In the intervening years, I had come out, been through two partners, was on to the third, and the house I shared with two gay men was a de facto office for the Gay

Solidarity Group. Kids and families were not part of our lives or the lives of most of the gay men and lesbians with whom I socialised or campaigned. As good Marxist feminist gay men, we were staunchly anti-patriarchy and anti-marriage. There were a couple of activists I knew who had been married and had kids before coming out, but the kids lived with their mothers, and while the dads would visit them, those kids were not part of their fathers' gay lives.

Dianne knew all of this, so I was ever so slightly fazed by her call. Thankfully, she assured me that we wouldn't have to fuck; the kid would be turkey-basted. She didn't want any financial support for the child: she did want the child to know I was the father and for me to have a part in the child's life as it grew, but she wasn't interested in forming a family with me.

I said 'yes'. And so it began.

Dianne kept track of her menstrual cycle and when she was ovulating I would get a call. She'd come over to my place and hang around in the kitchen while my partner Robert and I had non-penetrative sex in the bedroom. I would dutifully collect my sperm in one of those urine sample jars from the chemist, then Dianne would take it into another bedroom and inject it into her vagina. She used the turkey baster a couple of times but it was cumbersome so she soon switched to a plastic syringe. When she figured the sperm were happily on their journey and not likely to turn around and dribble out again, we'd all have a cup of tea and cake, and Dianne would head off till the next time.

Things were going as normally as they could under the circumstances, and then came the second fateful phone call.

Louise, a lesbian I knew through Robert, asked if I would be one of a quartet of donors for her and her partner Margaret. At that time, lesbians wanting to have a child had two choices: either pretend to be a straight woman with a husband who was infertile if they wanted to access costly IVF from an anonymous sperm donor bank, or find a man who would be a donor on their terms. In their case, they would raise the child themselves and expected no financial help from the successful donor. But they did want the child to know the donor and have contact with him when the child wanted it. I said 'yes' as a consciously political act.

Dianne became pregnant and we settled down into watching and waiting mode. I'd get calls telling me how things were going, and occasionally a grainy black-and-white ultrasound picture which just looked to me like a radar screen tracking some weather event. Meanwhile, Louise had been having trouble with the reliability of her other donors. When she heard that Dianne was pregnant, she decided to keep me on as the only one. She was also delighted by the prospect of a child with built-in sun protection.

And that's when things started to get very interesting for all of us.

Louise and Margaret asked to meet Dianne, because they wanted their child to know that Dianne's child was their child's sibling, and for them to spend time with each other. Although it was uncharted territory, we were embarking on an extended family of choice. Our joint commitment was to keep talking and working things out, particularly once the kids were born and started to have wishes of their own about the kinds of relationships they wanted with each other and with us. We agreed that the best approach was to answer the kids' questions honestly, as appropriate to their age.

Meanwhile, things were getting a little strange on Dianne's side of the family. Her sister was worried that their elderly mum wouldn't accept a grandchild born out of wedlock. So on Valentine's Day, six months into her pregnancy, Dianne rang me. Now, apparently, Valentine's Day is the only day on which a woman can ask a man to marry her. If the man refuses, he has to buy the woman a dozen pairs of white gloves. At least that's the story Dianne told me and we didn't have Wikipedia back then, so I couldn't confirm or deny it. I was a cheapskate and went for marriage.

We had two ceremonies, the first a more conservative affair at the Registry Office with her sister and brother-in-law, my parents and Robert as the witnesses; then a queer ceremony with Mother Inferior of the Sisters of Perpetual Indulgence as celebrant, the highlight of which was a gay friend of mine in a gorgeous white wedding dress throwing himself at my feet shouting 'It should've been me!' as he birthed a champagne bottle from under his dress.

Three months later, Mary was born. When the very long labour was over, Dianne was so exhausted that after a quick cuddle and bonding she handed Mary over to me and went to sleep. So there I was, a gay man in a birthing room, with a child I had never expected to have, never particularly wanted to have, but was absolutely entranced by. A child I now wanted very much indeed.

Rajendra, Louise's son, was born five months after Mary. I saw him the day after he was born and, again, I was besotted from the first look.

Word now was out that I was a reliable donor and soon I was donating to other lesbians. Usually the sperm was collected from my place in a transaction that lasted about as long as a pizza delivery, but in reverse. If I went to the woman's place to donate, they would sometimes have gay male porn on the bedside table just in case I was having an off day. I never asked what they did with it after I left.

Once I found myself donating to a woman whose cycle was totally out of whack. I jerked off seven nights in a row, which to be frank was more often than I was having sex at that time. I was so emotionally exhausted by the end of it that when I saw a TV news clip about a pod of whales and their babies stranded on a beach I broke into uncontrollable sobbing. Jerking off on demand is really, really draining. I don't know how porn stars do it. And I wasn't even being paid!

I wasn't asked to have a role in the life of any of the children who might be born from this new round of donations. They were not going to know their siblings, or be part of this extended family we had made. I don't even know if any or how many were born, except in one case where the mothers asked me for a picture that the child could have when she was curious about her donor. When she was born, they sent me a picture of her in return, but no contact details, as we had agreed. I was fine with all of this. While I was enjoying the growing relationships with Mary and Rajendra and, to be honest, enjoyed the social cachet of the transgressive extended family we had formed, I was clear that donoring was not about me and my needs. It was about the women and what they needed.

None of us knew it at the time, but we were having our children in the early years of the AIDS epidemic in Sydney. The guy I lost my gay virginity to died of an AIDS-related illness; so did my first partner; so did a few casual fucks; and so did one of Louise's other donors.

By the time Kerry and Simon asked me to be their donor, there was a test for HIV. Simon was infertile. They ruled out using an IVF clinic as it was too expensive and also because they wanted their child to know its donor father and to have contact with him on their terms. I was a work colleague of theirs; they knew about my donoring and that they could trust me to stick to agreements about contact. Fortunately, my HIV test came back negative. Alexis was born five years after Raj. And so our family grew.

Then, that same year, Louise and Margaret asked me to donate again. By now being a dad was a total buzz, so I said 'yes'. This time round I would go to their house for the drop off. Five-year-old Raj used to wonder why I would come over, play with him for a while, have dinner, then need a nap straight after. He was even more perplexed that his mum would need a nap straight after that. The line was that I was tired from the long drive. Jesse was the result of those naps.

We all settled into being this 'modern family'. We'd get together for the kids' birthdays, for Father's Day, to go watch the latest Pixar or Miyazaki. The mothers helped the kids negotiate the minefield that is the classroom and playground in a relentlessly heterosexual world. And the kids were growing up more than alright.

Then, ten years after Jesse was born, I got a call from Bronwyn, a heterosexual friend of mine. She was planning to have a child with a gay friend of hers and wanted to talk with me about what to discuss with the guy, how to approach the whole process. By now I had a bit of a reputation. I was 'donor central'.

We arranged to meet for coffee. When I turned up she told me that the prospective donor had gotten cold feet and backed out. We talked about how disappointing that was and how much she had already gone through in getting to this stage. Empathising with her plight, and more than happy to keep the family growing, I told her that if she liked I would be her donor instead. About eighteen months later, my youngest son Arlo was born. Bronwyn wanted Arlo to know I was his dad and to know and interact with his siblings. And so our family was again extended.

But while my family of choice had grown in such complex and wonderful ways, my birth family were still left in the dark. Apart from my youngest brother, my birth family still only knew about Mary, the child born in 'wedlock' to Dianne and me. My parents looked after her from time to time when she was young and she was very much their grandchild. I was forty-seven now, and my dad was turning eighty. Although we had had some difficult times over the years, we had grown increasingly close and I wanted him to meet his other grandchildren. So, with everyone's agreement, after a birthday yum cha with my parents, my brothers and their wives, I told my dad I had a special birthday present for him. I put pictures of all the kids on the table one at a time, like a gambler in a Kenny Rogers song. And with each picture his smile broadened. That year at our annual Boxing Day get-together, my parents met all of their grandchildren and their grandchildren's parents.

Not long after, I featured in an episode of *Australian Story* on the ABC called 'Father's Day'. Mary and Raj and Bronwyn took part. It was a very public coming out for me as a donor dad and for them as 'gaybies' – though we didn't use that term at the time. Jesse was in his last years of high school, where he wasn't open about his conception or about me. The day before the episode screened, he told his closest friends, all of whom were totally supportive.

And so began the next phase of the story, this time a story being told by the kids. Jesse and Raj went on to take part in the first version of Maya Newell's film *Gayby Baby*, a documentary screened on the ABC. Raj got involved with the promotion and distribution of the feature-length version of the film, and went down to Canberra for a panel discussion, speaking directly to politicians at Parliament House, advocating for the rights of his family. Alexis, Kerry, Simon and I were filmed for a Japanese TV documentary on sperm donation, and Alexis and I were on the SBS *Insight* episode on donor parenting. And in 2017,

Jesse appeared on the gaybies episode of *You Can't Ask That* on ABC TV. Raj, now a television producer, lamented that we had missed the opportunity for a reality TV show to rival the Kardashians.

Well, Raj, there is still time. Family is a never-ending story, and as long as the bomb-happy current crop of world leaders don't wipe us all out in the next couple of years, I have my grand-gayby-babies to look forward to.

'But, Paul,' you say, 'what about this marriage business? Where did you anti-patriarchy parents all go so terribly wrong?' I don't think we did. We brought up our kids to make their own decisions and if getting married is one of them, that's fine with me. Even married married. After being accepted by my family despite all of my weirdness, it would be pretty naff of me not to accept my kids, no matter how weird I may find their choices.

Paul van Reyk

Paul van Reyk was born in Sri Lanka in 1952, migrating to Australia with his family in 1962. He came out publicly in 1978, and has spent the subsequent four decades as an activist. He has been a regular media commentator over that time, writing on gay and HIV/AIDS history, racism in the gay community and LGBTQIA+ families, and he has performed monologues on his life as an activist and gay donor dad.

A social worker by profession, Paul also manages his own consultancy company, and blogs regularly about food, family, activism and his dogs.

GEN(D)ERATIONS

Mama Alto

The edges of the foldaway bed hold a strange fascination for me: the soft foam of the mattress, lovingly swaddled in a worn, cotton bed sheet many times older than I am, meets the cold, hard, metal springs and bars which comprise the bed's frame. I am perhaps three or four years of age, maybe five, and the temporary, portable bed sits at the end of the queen size bed where my grandmother and grandfather will sleep – in this stranger's home that they rent when they visit us from interstate.

My sister, also older than me, sleeps in the next room over; we are spending the night here, a short walk away from our parent's home. We spent the day sweeping leaves in the small courtyard, pretending to be Snow White or Cinderella, with our grandfather laughing that in our fantasy lives as princesses we are enacting servant tasks. He gives me a small, soft, toy football. 'Soon you can learn to play footy,' he says, and chuckles.

'Boys can't be princesses.' He smiles encouragingly, generously, and I feel brave, but still I look down grimly as he places this small bomb into my reluctantly outstretched palm, my sister nearby happily humming to herself as she sweeps.

•

Backstage, I am peering into the mirror. The light bulbs are bright along its frame, and I am taming my long wavy hair into shape for the show, pinning it into curls with white gardenias, singing softly to myself. I think about dreams and fantasies and how on earth I came to be sitting here, about to go on at a beautiful theatre, to be blessed with the honour of singing to people. I gently glide across the dressing room to the costume rack and remove my gown for the evening from the crinkly black plastic dry-cleaning bag. It emerges like an exquisite insect from a cocoon, sparkling softly in the blinding mirror light and shimmering gently from the hum of the air conditioning. I step into the dress and feel the cares of the day begin to slip away.

Returning to the mirror, I make small finishing touches to my make-up, and the weight of my daily battles recedes as the power that is glamour empowers my heart, one dab of eye shadow at a time. I think about the train trip earlier that day, the older men who stared as I boarded and coughed under their breath, 'Faggot'. The small child at the station who asked his mother, 'Is that a man or a lady?' The mother stiffening and tightening her grip on the child's schoolbag, hissing, 'Just don't talk to her.'

I remember the walk to the theatre, where a man my age spat on the ground in front of my feet. He met my eye with the horrific gaze of a person who knows that they control the world. The entitlement and power and privilege to do what he pleases, to whom he pleases, and to get away with it. I thought about saying something. I didn't. I stopped the tears from welling up and I kept walking. He trailed me almost all the way to the theatre, making sure I knew that he belonged in this world and I did not.

I ignore the heavy newspaper in my bag and the typed print within it that condemns and ridicules me. Gross gender confusion. Freakish. Unnatural. As I gently paint on one last layer of lipstick, I feel the bitterness transform. I look into the mirror at the goddess I can be – not something I paint on, but something that is always inside me. I hear the excited and apprehensive murmur of the audience as they take their seats. I stand, breathe deep, and think of all the divas who came before me. Power and love surround me as I prepare to step onto the stage. I remember one last thing, and turn back to the mirror. I fix my hair, spraying the curls and flowers and pins into place with a solid layer of hairspray.

•

Lying there in the foldaway bed, I think about earlier that morning. My grandmother fixing her hair in the bathroom mirror, using her enormous hairspray can, encased in a pink reminiscent of Jackie Kennedy's pillbox hat, with an equally vintage-style typography. The spray had a distinctive smell, noxious but comforting. Like the hairspray can, my grandmother has a fascinating mystique – sophisticated but mysterious, elegant but everyday. I would follow her around the house watching her elaborate morning rituals.

Watching her neatly and deftly styling waves into her thick silver hair, I absentmindedly sit atop the waste bin lid. Catching sight of me in the mirror, fearing for my life and the stability of the bin, she pivots around on one sensibly heeled shoe and swoops me up off the lid and onto the tiles. 'Now, now, you won't be able to sit there for much longer – you're getting to be a big boy now!' I cross my arms and my face feels hot and flushed. I shake my head and burst into tears and, perplexed, she strokes my hair. Later I hear her talking to my grandfather while I pretend to be asleep in the foldaway bed: 'I just don't know quite what upset him, but I think he must have heard his dad tell his sister that she's a big girl, and that there are jobs and responsibilities that come with being big and grown-up. I think he got upset when I used the word "big". I can't think what else it could have been.'

•

I open my mouth and the first notes fly from my throat. The stage lights blind my vision slightly, blurring the audience, but I am comfortable here. It is familiar and warm. I am in control. I am a songstress and a princess and a diva. The notes resonate into the theatre. High, clear and soprano, they mellow into my huskier and weaker alto tones before mellifluously soaring back once more into the highest realms. I hear audible gasps in the audience. It is that first electric moment of my show where I always feel the audience shift. They cannot place the gender. Some are curious; some horrified; some intrigued. The gentle make-up, the hair in tight curls and pinned with flowers, the luscious gown – these all suggest the feminine; but in the shapes of the body, the jawline, the speaking voice, perhaps, some people can see something masculine.

But the singing? The singing occupies some other place. Somewhere between or beyond genders. High and feminine, but it is not quite a female voice. Yet it cannot reach the depths of the male baritone or tenor. 'Countertenor', the classical music historians and pedagogues from my past whisper, in scandalised sotto voce, as though it is a dirty word, but I am lifted by the music into another place and time, and dismiss any thought of science or of theory, of gendered constructions to neatly categorise the voice types across binaries or dichotomies.

The applause rings through the theatre at the end of the first song, and I pause to take in what I can through my spotlight-blurry vision. I see friends and family but mostly strangers. I gently smooth out the flowing folds and gathered fabrics of the gown and I smile, holding out my arms to welcome the audience. A distinguished but very elderly and very frail lady who I don't know, sitting in the front row, cheers. I blow her a kiss and she catches it, delighted, as the pianist begins the second song.

•

In the morning, my grandfather is the first one to wake up. He moves quietly around the house, first turning on the heaters, next opening the blinds. Fixing the breakfasts, boiling the kettle, running the water in the bathroom until it runs hot so that my grandmother's bath will be warm enough. I try to sneakily roll from the little bed onto the floor, and gently pad on socked feet across the hallway on my secretive mission. My grandmother watches with silent amusement from her neatly structured array of pillows as I crash around. I tug my grandfather's arm as he strolls back towards the bedroom, holding two bowls of cereal, and he looks down with love. 'Today,' I ask, 'can you pretend I am a little granddaughter?' His face furrows – confusion and concern. Very quietly, he says, 'That's a bit silly.' He walks into the bedroom and hands a bowl to my grandmother, kissing her on the forehead. 'Your hair looks nice today!' As he says it, she beams. My sister sleepily enters the room and sits on the edge of the mattress. I silently decide to never again speak out loud the idea that I might be anything other than a boy.

•

The foyer is abuzz with noise and life as I enter from the theatre, and the distinguished elderly lady from the front row is propped up on her walking frame. The wheels of the frame gently rock back and forth like the tide. She is sobbing openly, and I cautiously approach. As she sights me, her face lights up through her tears, and she lets go of the walking frame. It happily rolls away of its own accord, and the woman's daughter dashes after it. The elderly lady grabs hold of my arm – at first, I think, for balance. I have changed from the gown into a beaded bolero jacket, and my hair has begun to unravel from the tight curls and flower pins. She sighs, looking at her hand as it presses into the sequins of my sleeve. I can't help but wonder what she is thinking as I help her into a chair. She begins to speak.

•

That day, after my grandmother has fixed her hair and walks from the bathroom to the kitchen, I linger by the vanity. I carefully pick up the hairspray can and try to quietly spray a small amount into the air. I close my eyes and breathe in that strange breeze, imagining that I might be someone else. I open my eyes and catch a glimpse of myself in the hand mirror, a strangely magical contraption that magnifies the face across a concave surface. Eyeing my distorted reflection suspiciously, I wonder if anyone would understand the strange way I feel about the short-haired boy glaring back at me. I push the hand mirror face down on the table and scamper to follow my grandmother.

•

The lady settles into the chair, and begins to tell me her life story, starting with her humble upbringing in a small village. Her religious parents. The invasion of their village. The march. The camp. The death and destruction. Her miraculous survival. Her long lost uncle, a musician, who came to her rescue after the war. 'When I hear music,' she says, 'I remember him.' She begins to sob once more, but retains a beautifully articulate manner of speaking through her emotion. 'After the war, I was so traumatised I could not speak. But he was a clever man, my uncle, and instead of trying to talk with me, he played me music. He took me to concerts. He took me to see singers. And it healed me until I could speak. I was just a little girl. And these people filled with so much hatred for someone, just because they are different . . .'

The depth of her emotions and the weight of history overwhelm her, and her voice begins to crackle and croak. Her tears amplify and she struggles for breath as she looks into my eyes. Her daughter, waiting nearby with the renegade walking frame, begins to rush forward but the lady holds up a firm palm to dismiss her. She looks into my eyes again: 'People can hold so, so much hatred for someone just because they are different. And you. You are there, singing – the music that reminds me of my uncle. And you are beautiful. Whether you are a beautiful woman, or a beautiful man, or neither – I really don't know, but . . .' She pauses to think. 'But I don't care. It doesn't matter. What matters is that no one can decide that for you. No one! Never let anyone choose for you. Only you can choose. Never, never let anyone else tell you who you are.'

She takes a heavy breath and her hand reaches once more for the sequins of my jacket. As my last few curls fall from their flower pins, I can smell a faint trace of hairspray rising from me. It is noxious, but comforting. She closes her eyes and quietly hums a half-forgotten song.

Mama Alto

Mama Alto is a gender transcendent diva, cabaret artiste, jazz singer and community activist based in Melbourne. She is a non-binary trans femme person of colour who works with the radical potential of storytelling, strength in softness and power in vulnerability. Mama's cabaret performances and collaborations have garnered critical praise at venues and festivals including the Melbourne Recital Centre, the National Theatre Melbourne, Malthouse Theatre Company, Griffin Theatre Company, Melbourne Festival, Adelaide Fringe Festival, Adelaide Cabaret Festival, Darwin Festival, Havana International Theatre Festival, Marysville Jazz and Blues Weekend, Melbourne Cabaret Festival, Stonnington Jazz Festival, and Wonderland (Brisbane).

Mama Alto was the delighted recipient of the 2014 Weekly Award for Best Cabaret at Adelaide Fringe, the 2016 Arts Access Victoria Outstanding Access & Inclusion Award at Melbourne Fringe, and the 2017 Artist of the Year Award at the GLOBE LGBTI Awards.

COMING OUT

Benjamin Law

As time goes on, I'm not sure how I feel about the term – or the concept of – 'coming out'. To me, it's always sounded vaguely sinister. Or graphic. 'Coming out.' It sounds like you're talking about poo. And, like the torrent of hungover shit that streams forth after your first Mardi Gras party, coming out is kind of exhausting.

It is always a fraught process, a delicate art of choosing the right timing (not Christmas) and situation (not public transport). And it's an ongoing process too: every time we make a new friend or get a new job, we have to somehow subtly convey that we're not actually heterosexual. Unless we're draped with a rainbow banner or have pink triangles flying out of our arseholes, we are constantly spelling it out to people, day in, day out.

What amplifies our exhaustion is how awkward people feel around us. 'I'm gay,' we might say. Or trans, or lesbian, or bisexual – whatever. Now we watch as their tongues become knotted. Witness their brains melting; their systems shutting down. Only months later, with the benefit of hindsight, will they realise what they should've said all along ('That's okay; you're the same person to me'), rather than the mumbling, soul-destroying comments they made at the time: 'Really?'; 'Are you sure?'; 'But you've dated dudes/chicks before!'; 'But you enjoy sports'; and an all-time favourite: 'What if you get AIDS and die all alone?'

When my friend Kirk (not his real name) came out to his mother, the first thing she said was, 'Never tell your father.' The second thing: 'You don't like little boys too, do you?' Afterwards, his father said how he would have to start thinking of Kirk more as a daughter now. Other friends have stories of parents reading their homoerotic diaries before banning them from pursuing drama classes. A friend's mother confronted him by printing out all his gay internet porn and reclining on his bed, waiting for his return. A few years back, a Rockhampton father made the news for forcing his fourteen-year-old son to sleep with a female sex worker after suspecting he was gay; yes, this actually happened in the twenty-first century.

I'm lucky enough to be able to look back and genuinely say I'm fond of my coming out story. I was seventeen at the time – and I'd spent my entire childhood in the state of Queensland, which, at any given moment, is either the most regressive or progressive state in the country. It's kind of nuts.

You might laugh at the idea of Queensland – cradle of Katter, hellmouth of Hanson – being a progressive stronghold, but keep in mind we are the only state to have directly elected not just one, but two women premiers; no other female premier in Australia has ever been elected directly into office by voters. On the other hand, we're the only mainland state to have no legal nude beaches, *American Psycho* still technically needs to be sold in shrink-wrap, we held off on fluoride in our water for decades (the only thing worse than a British smile is a Queensland one) and we were the last mainland state to decriminalise homosexuality – in 1990, when I was eight years old.

Throughout childhood, I'd watch state politicians rail against the evils of homosexuality on TV, saying that gays were perverted, that they were all involved in extreme sex acts like scat play and fisting and were degenerates because they couldn't reproduce. In my now enlightened adulthood, I know that extreme sex acts aren't prerequisites to being homosexual, just as extreme childbirth isn't a prerequisite to being heterosexual. In any case, childbirth is basically being fisted, in reverse, by a miniature human head.

WHO'S THE SICKO NOW, I ASK YOU?

My point is, for a significant period of my childhood, the adult I would grow up to be was criminalised by the state. And by the time I was in high school – a conservative, Lutheran private school where all the cool kids were super-straight surfers – being gay was still considered the worst thing you could be.

And so at age seventeen – about to leave home, and having managed chronic anxiety and panic attacks for my entire teens – I decided to come out as gay to Mum, more out of exhaustion than anything else. There is nothing more tiring than hiding a key aspect of your identity 24/7, and I did not have much energy as a teenager anyway.

One night, after I'd graduated but before I moved out of home, I said I had something important to tell her, then burst into tears. And I don't cry in that very dignified Cate-Blanchett-on-the-big-screen way. My crying is snotty and ugly, and I sound like a small dog whimpering after being kicked repeatedly.

'What's the problem?' Mum asked.

'I ha-ave some-thi-ing,' I choked, 'to tell you.'

She looked concerned. 'Are you on drugs?'

I shook my head.

'Have you gotten someone pregnant?'

Mmm, colder, I thought.

'No!' I said.

'Um . . .' Mum said, as though she was on a game show. 'Ooooh, I know, I know! You're gay.'

When I nodded, worried about her reaction, she put a hand to her chest and patted me.

'Well, what's wrong with that?' Mum asked. 'There's nothing wrong with being gay.'

I looked up at her, surprised. 'Really?'

'Gay people can't help it,' she said. 'It just means that something went wrong in the womb, that's all.'

Recently, I reminded Mum of this conversation and she stood by it. 'Ai,' she said. 'There's no scientific proof of why people are gay. Probably the surgeon cleaned too much stuff out after the miscarriage I had before you, scraped too many hormones out or something.'

After that I came out to my two older siblings. Then my two younger siblings. Only years and years later did I come out to my Dad. It wasn't my intention to leave him out of the loop; it's just that he was more a traditional Chinese guy, and we rarely talked about our private lives. He was the kind of divorced father who – in the process of not living in the same house with me any longer – had lost all concept of the kind of person I'd become. Poor Dad: he'd call me out of the blue every fortnight, then when we'd covered the usual territory (my degree, his business, the weather, my grandmother's health), he'd get flustered, say he didn't want to disturb me any longer and end the call there. But then a Thai guy started working at his restaurant – gorgeous, young and utterly flaming – and before long became Dad's 2IC. I figured that if Dad was okay with Narweng, he might possibly be okay with me.

After I told him, there was silence. 'Does your mother know?' he eventually said.

'Yes,' I said.

'And your older sister? She knows?'

'Yes, Dad,' I said, feeling bad he was so far down the line.

He looked straight ahead, thinking.

'And your older brother? He knows?'

'Yes, Dad.'

A long pause.

'And your younger sister, she knows?'

Oh for fuck's sake, I thought.

Now emboldened, the comings out didn't stop there. After that, I'd come out to all sorts of people. To taxi drivers. Hotel reservation staff. New colleagues. Extended relatives. Some arsehole waiter taking my order. Coming out, as every queer person eventually learns, isn't a single moment. We spend the rest of our lives coming out.

And so cut to 2017, a few thousand comings out later. It was the end of a long week, and my boyfriend and I were furiously packing bags to fly interstate. Two of my sisters had birthdays – Candy's 40th, Tammy's 30th – and they'd booked a house on Stradbroke, an island only accessible by barge. Everyone was coming: my divorced parents, all five siblings, myriad partners. It was supposed to be fun, but in a post-nuclear family like ours, trips like these can spell possible fallout. 'Just letting you know,' Tammy texted me, 'Ma-Ma is staying too. A reminder for you and Scott ;)'.

'Wait, your grandma's coming?' Scott, my partner, said.

Fuck. Clearly I hadn't read the itinerary properly. I came out to Mum half a lifetime ago, but I'd never come out to my Ma-Ma, my dad's mum and last living grandparent. She was coming to Stradbroke and Scott would be there too.

It's partly cultural (that unquestioned Chinese expectation to marry), partly generational (she's eighty-eight) and partly to do with language. My spoken Cantonese is so appalling, I wouldn't know where to start. My family were also ambivalent. 'I don't know,' Dad would say. 'How would she react?'

my siblings would say. 'What if she had a heart attack?' Mum would say. All very helpful.

So I had left it. It was easier to deflect Ma-Ma's questions – 'I'm too busy to have girlfriends; you got any boyfriends?' – than to tell her the truth and potentially spoil a rare evening together. Inevitably I'd go home miserable, feeling the full weight of the cop-out, but the feeling would pass as I got back to my daily gay existence. Now, though, the prospect of a weekend together having to pretend exhausted me. It wasn't the 1950s anymore. Scott wasn't a 'flatmate' and she deserved to know.

'Ugh, I'm just going to tell her,' I said, zipping our bags.

'Seriously?' he said, chasing after me.

'She's eighty-eight. I'm sure she's lived through worse.'

I texted my family to let them know. I could tell they were worried when they didn't text back.

That night, after dinner, everyone played board games while Ma-Ma and I quietly watched.

'You're doing so well with work now,' she said. 'Now all you need to do is find a wife.'

I sighed and smiled weakly, two wines in.

'Ma-Ma,' I said, taking her hand and speaking clumsily in Cantonese in what I imagine must've sounded like an inexplicably thick Russian accent to her. 'I will not be doing the marriage.'

She shot me a look and slapped my thigh. 'What? Don't be silly.'

'I be not the silly,' I said. 'I not like the women.'

She slapped my thigh again. 'What are you talking about?'

'That white ghost devil over there,' I said, pointing to Scott. 'He be my boyfriend.'

We queers are a diverse bunch – transgender, lesbian, intersex, bi, gay – ostensibly, on paper, we don't have that much in common. But what many of us do share is a period of hiding and a moment of fear, when we need to clarify, correct or bail someone up. The moment of revelation. Most of us would have – at some point – had to tell people that their assumptions about us were wrong.

But if I've learnt anything in my years of comings out, it's that if people care, what they mostly need is reassurance.

'But you know something?' I said. 'Me happy. You happy too, Ma-Ma?'

Ma-Ma thought about it and scanned the room: this sprawling family she'd made, all their partners, and this grandson who wrote stories she'd never read. She patted my hand.

'Well then,' she said. 'I'm happy too.'

And though there's still confusion now – my Chinese grandmother, though she knows I'm in a relationship with Scott, doesn't see why us being in a committed gay relationship should prevent either of us from getting married to women – I feel lighter. And the next day, floating in the sea, as I told my siblings the story of me coming out again, I was happy too, and, for so many reasons, feeling seventeen again.

Benjamin Law

Benjamin Law writes books, TV screenplays, columns, essays and feature journalism. He's the author of *The Family Law* (2010), *Gaysia: Adventures in* the *Queer East* (2012) and the Quarterly Essay on Safe Schools, *Moral Panic 101* (2017).

The Family Law is now an award-winning TV series for SBS, which Benjamin created and co-writes. He also co-hosts ABC RN's weekly pop culture show *Stop Everything*.

Parts of this essay were previously published in Good Weekend *magazine.*

KNOWING AND UNKNOWING

Liz Duck-Chong

I want to tell you a story of gender, and of the process of storytelling itself.

It takes place in several parts, spread across a lifetime, and it happens with very little thought as to what will happen next, as life tends to. There are no illusions that it is not a story about me, but we will figure out how exactly this is the case later. Most of all, it is a story just for you.

This story takes place when a child is born and given an identity and a set of pronouns. This process is crucial, and people celebrate and reward this unveiling. She is brought into a world that won't understand her for a long time, and that will admonish her for that very lack of understanding. A bouquet of balloons deflates in a corner over subsequent months, wrinkling until the blue is barely discernible amidst the chaos of bringing a newborn child home.

This story takes place in early primary school, in a grade one room she remembers vividly. At the front of the class, a boy and a girl identify and carefully name the respective caricature genitals on cartoon bodies for the whole class, and there's no longer any denying that there exists a polarity of being. The room is lit up with embarrassed giggles, but a young girl sees her own body illustrated, beneath the pointed finger of the boy, and knows immediately she isn't like the others. Many years later, she too points fingers, invoking this moment as proof.

It takes place at the start of her teens, her body ensnared in the insidious tendrils of unwanted puberty, a landscape beneath her shifting and changing in ways she had neither been warned about nor feared nearly enough. The undoing of a sense of safety occurs, one that had previously extended up until the point where her body stopped, now stopping far shorter. She pictures her body as one big semi-permeable membrane, a term recently learned, and testosterone as the lethal chemical that can trespass beyond her walls, an enemy from within. She starts the descent into uncertainty and vulnerability, alternating between being afraid she will lose her mind and assuming she has lost it already.

It takes place towards the end of high school, talking to an ongoing escalation of doctors about her changing body, her regret, her grief. This is a process of proving herself, like a test for a life, she recalls in acute detail. She mumbles the word 'transsexual', and seeks the freedom of diagnosis; the word 'torment' comes to her mind and her lips, crying off her eyeliner as it is spoken. A psychiatrist grants her a treatment plan after a great deal of deliberation. It is black and white, and she adjusts so that the corners can find a comfortable place inside her softening body.

It takes place as a young woman confronts a world that has few places for her, and fewer still she mustn't fight to exist in. Even now, outing herself to medical professionals and employers, well aware of the keys that they keep a hold of, she tells these stories to them all just like this. She describes her body as held back, uncomfortable, traumatic; her language intricate, demurred and precise. She takes on the process of recounting these memories over and over, until they blend together and become indistinguishable from all the stories she has heard.

•

Queer is knowing and not knowing. All these stories are real stories; they are my stories, and many others', without a doubt, but they aren't the whole story, not yet. As queers, as individuals and communities, we're expected to live certain narratives, fit certain archetypes. We are then expected to not only behave accordingly, but far better. When I am the good trans woman, I smile with my teeth, I show a little cleavage as proof, I struggle to feign excitement on weekday morning TV about Caitlyn Jenner coming out.

But I'm not always the good trans woman – an idea as impossible as it is exhausting – and so I tell you these stories as part of an unreliable history of me. To simply have one telling is too simple, but also far too boring, requiring the restraint and restructuring of parts of us that deserve to see light. Queer is as much an unknowableness of self as it is an identity; a constant analysis, and an internal call and response. My narration is as unreliable as my intentions in writing this down, and so we continue down this garden path.

•

This part of the story also takes place when a child is born, although maybe the surrounding details are less important. There is talk of the sex, and even in the OshKosh haze of the 1990s children are colour-coded for ease of identification. Despite this, people seem as entranced by her hands and feet, her belly and fingernails and soft head, as they are by other parts of her. A binary of language springs up around her out of automatic ease, but her parents have a hard enough time finding even a single word to describe the enormity of what they've embarked upon, and there is a beauty also in the not having of words.

It takes place in early primary school, as outside each classroom is marked a boys' line and a girls' line, still a clear demarcation, but sometimes someone has to cross from one to the other to even out numbers, and no one bats an eye at this simple act. She feels different, but outside an acceptable range of difference; not an either/or but an additional and, a distinction the first telling of the story has no room for. She remains unsure as to why boys don't get to wear dresses and skirts, but because they look comfortable, not out of some deep yearning. Sometimes she enjoys wearing shorts too, but it will be many years before she realises it's just potentially not about clothing. She forgets about her discomfort for years at a time, too busy being curious about the world around her, and maybe that's okay too.

This story takes place in her early teens, as she enters into what will become a first puberty, hormones coursing through her, not feeling the pure fear of the last telling, but still confused and concerned about what the future holds for her. She isn't positive about the rigidity and foreignness that being 'born in the wrong body' describes, yet her body increasingly doesn't fit right. She finds Bailey Jay's pornography online late at night and realises that other women like her are out there. She is learning how to exist under the male gaze alongside her peers, despite vastly different bodies. One day she will read the words 'My body is not the source of my oppression. Men are the source of my oppression' and it will resonate deeply within her, but for now she finds an uncomplicated sisterhood within small online communities who are overjoyed to see her truth, passing advice down a chain reaching back further than she could possibly know.

It takes place towards the end of high school, as she makes friends and trusts them enough to share secrets previously unspoken. She whispers the word 'transgender' to two girls in a lighting booth bathed all in blue, sisters except by blood. They hold her like they would any other girl. In secret they use her name, gift her old clothes, do her face in the dead of night and take her out, and for the first time she feels the sun on a face that looks like how it does in her head. There is increasingly light in her life, and it forms ever new shades of grey, some murky but some soft and forgiving.

It takes place as she grows older, finding her place in a community of women who breathe life into the embers of art and passion she has struggled to keep lit. She takes strength from the way they trust and invite her in, even if they do sometimes fuck up her pronouns. She also discovers other trans women, their presence kicking out the walls of her understanding and their friendships some of the most important she will know. Increasingly, she tells these stories to them just like this. Her language is loose, still uncomfortable, and definitely grammatically incorrect, but it sounds so good rolled around in the mouths of others.

•

These stories are real stories, and they are still incomplete, yet now we're starting to see into their depth. A story, like a memory, isn't stationary; for it to sit preserved forever would allow us no impermanence, no growth. We tell stories in order to be known, to know ourselves, and knowing one's self isn't a process that ends easily. They alter as we require them to, shifting between the known and the unknown, as we remember new details or misremember old ones, diminishing or embellishing them for our readers.

There can never remain one capital-T Truth when we are multitudes of truths wrapped up in this queer skin, so very permeable, so easily bruised, but so willingly shared. Like a spring-laden branch, the deadnames my friends, lovers and family were once known by have been replaced by new and beautiful ones, and the stories that accompany them taste far sweeter than last season's. It doesn't diminish us to acknowledge these truths, these flavours; rather, it shows how we truly exist, brilliant and boundless. And so with appetites stoked, we continue with our story.

•

This part of the story too takes place when the same child is born, or slightly beforehand; it's indistinct and irrelevant at this point in the telling. The important part is that there is now something that once wasn't, and this holds a lot of meaning to a small constellation of people. As parents are wont to do, her parents impart a great many hopes and fears onto a growing cluster of cells. One day this child will reject some of these, including ones their parents didn't ever expect her to reject, but when has a person ever grown up to perfectly satisfy the expectations of those around them? Where is the joy in ever being fully formed? They find themselves loved, regardless, and give thanks for this every day.

It takes place in early primary school. She's standing under a tree in the playground with a friend from the year above her, the memory seared into her mind ever since. He's reading a newly acquired *Guinness Book of Records* and points agape at the winner for 'Greatest number of sex change operations performed by one person'. Even armed only with their bare minimum sex education, he is disgusted. He asks, 'Who would ever want that?' and she thinks and genuinely imagines 'Hey, maybe I would.' But she also wants a green lightsaber like the one Luke Skywalker built and a secret underground bunker and to be a mermaid, so when people point to these experiences as some sort of proof, she will look back and laugh at the wide eyes of a child assessing their options, happy at the freedom she was given to imagine so many possibilities.

It takes place at the start of her teens, not the contractual raging inferno of fear and transformation but rather just equal parts uncomfortable and curious about the ways bodies can change. She simultaneously clings to her girlhood while growing up all at once, aware of how things must go from here, running outcomes in her head and planning for the worst. She recounts after the fact that she is scared of her body, and how everyone around her says it is supposed to have sex, but her reality has far more to do with inclination, with pacing. One day, when she's ready, she'll share her first time with a friend who doesn't believe in the idea of virginities; who touches her face and calls her beautiful in a way that no one has before. She learns that body parts are far less important than everyone says they are, and she slowly opens up to others. She buys her first party frock. She is diagnosed with depression. She learns the joy of kissing other girls. She is not one plot line, and will never carry just one story arc with her.

It takes place towards the end of high school, and the labels that escape her mouth in late night whispers taste almost right, but by now she knows that it will always be a work in progress, an unfolding plot. She finds her style gradually, across Halloween parties and marriage equality rallies, slowly homing in on a hard-won sense of self. Her friends call her a mystery, and she laughs, knowing full well that as much is unknown to her as to them, but plays it close to a newly budding chest. It takes place as she comes of age, as she takes hold of what her body is becoming and is determined to call it her own.

It takes place over the years that follow, discovering that her wanting to be a woman is possibly the most boring thing about her, and instead focusing on what type of woman she wants to be – a far more rewarding question. It takes place inside and then outside of a closet not of her own design, but one she finds the strength to destroy; it takes place in marches and chatrooms and backyards and bedrooms as she reaches out to individuals, and to a growing community, and as they reach back with love, creating so much colour in her life. It takes place constantly, in the known and in the unknown.

It takes place here and now, as I write to you and as you read my words, wondering what comes next, and as I wonder with you. Our paths are aligned here for just this one moment, sharing this page with no respect for the boundaries of time and distance and circumstance. We gather here, in this instant, and this becomes a part of it; a part of us. We're learning to tell these stories together: just like this.

Liz Duck-Chong

Liz Duck-Chong is a writer, sexual health nerd, photographer and musician who almost exclusively wears odd socks. She has had her work featured in the *Sydney Morning Herald, Crikey, Meanjin, Kill Your Darlings, ABC Online, SBS Online, Archer Magazine, Junkee,* and *Overland.*

A proud trans and non-binary woman, Liz is a true renaissance figure in the sense that most of them were really gay. She can be found on **@lizduckchong** or co-hosting **@letsdoitpodcast**, a podcast about queer sexual health.

HOW TO MAKE YOUR BED

Maxine Kauter

It was a full moon and I was standing in a small shared courtyard out the back of my friend Dave's apartment. The air was summery, and a warm, blustery wind was chasing leaves in circles about the concrete ground. Inside I could hear the party chattering over music. There were about eight of us left and everyone but me was crowded on Dave's floor, laughing and talking shit. The smell of weed and tobacco danced in the air.

I was brooding. I was leaning against the red brick wall outside and looking up at a patch of sky between the towering buildings. Moonlit clouds were rushing by like a film on fast forward: a flowing river, a stampede of horses. Relentless images in the ether.

Suddenly, the wind died. The leaves fell lifeless to the ground and that rushing sky halted to a complete stop.

The clouds had arranged themselves into the image of a giant dragon face and that face filled the entire sky. From one of the dragon's eyes a sudden flash of coloured light shot out directly at me. When it hit me, I felt an intense euphoria. I was overcome by an otherworldly benevolence that had targeted me specifically. My entire body was buzzing, each and every cell charged with fuzzy, glittery joy. I was bursting with an important understanding of the universe that I couldn't quite put my finger on, like a dream on waking. I felt charged, rapturous.

After a moment the wind resumed and the clouds recommenced their rushing, obliterating the dragon face. But the euphoria and the benevolence remained.

The acid trip that I had taken was called a Purple Ohm. I got the Ohm. This story is about how that Ohm lasted for a good few years, taking me on an amazing adventure right into the heart of Pentecostal Christianity and teaching me that you should be careful how well you make your bed because you might find yourself asleep in it for a lot longer than you anticipate.

I was nineteen years old when I got the Ohm. I had just begun dating Deborah, my second ever girlfriend. I had a nice group of friends. I was smoking a lot of weed. Taking heaps of acid. I was reading, writing and making things. Life was pretty good. But when the sky dragon shot me down with her love-laden laser beam of colour I felt an intense need to leave that party.

Deborah lived in the apartment upstairs from Dave. The building provided housing to young people kicked out of home for being gay or trans. She took me to her flat and sat on the floor while I paced about the room babbling about the meaning of life and the universe. What I didn't know about Deborah was that she came from a very religious family and was struggling with terrible guilt about being a homosexual. She had also taken the Purple Ohm acid. When I got the Ohm, she took this as a sign that God was trying to bring her back to the fold. And she got the Ohm too. She pulled out a Bible and tried to show me that what I was having was something called a 'road to Damascus' experience.

I grew up in what I would call a culturally Catholic family. Easter, Christmas, schooling. A sort of 'in-name-only' secular Catholicism. So I knew the stories she was telling me. Virgin birth. Messiah. Blood baths. Rising from the dead. But her interpretation of these things was a lot friendlier than the Catholics'. In the weeks following the onset of the Ohm she reconnected with people she knew from church and they all tried to get me to attend.

The church was not like any I had ever been to. It met in a function room at the Coronation Club in Burwood.

We got the train there and it was then that I received another major revelation: Burwood is not in Penrith. We made our way through the entry, the sound of pokies as cloying as the smell of old deep-fryer oil. An old man. A perspex raffle box. A chocolate wheel. Sign-in books.

But upstairs, we were greeted by very clean people in tasteful clothing. An excessive hygiene hung about them. These people smiled warmly and looked me right in the eye like they were searching for something very important. They shook my hand and some of them did that two-handed handshake in which the handshake becomes a proxy hug. They repeated my name when I was introduced, as if using some learned technique to commit it, and me, to memory. Children ran around the place and their parents reined them in with a beneficent calm. They were kind, well-meaning people. I was terrified.

The room was arranged in rows of club seats facing a lectern. There was a band, with drums, and a singer who closed her eyes and lifted her enraptured face to the low-hung ceiling as if it were the great dome of the Hagia Sophia. In place of stained glass, there were stacks of superfluous chairs. Where an altar should be, there was an overhead projector showing us the words to sing.

A very short man got up in front of everyone and began speaking. Instead of robes, he wore that middle-of-the-road 'trendy' that you might find in General Pants. He went about explaining the gospel and his explanation was like a Radiohead song: just vague and confusing enough for me to impose my own meaning on it.

•

All this reminded me of my adolescence. I would lie on my bed listening to music and dreaming of a time when I would be old enough to go and find my people. These were not the people living in my home. These were not the people I went to school with. Not the people I played sports with. These were a fabled people. And when I found them, I would find that they were good: open-minded, worldly, kind and wholly superior to the people I knew now. They would be interested in the ideas I was interested in, and human prejudice; human failings would not be present in them.

I became saved.

To my legitimate surprise, people in the church were quite concerned about whether or not Deborah and I were sleeping together. In fact, being a practising homosexual was almost the only thing that was explicitly forbidden in the church. One thing you had to try really hard not to do. Having practising homosexuals in the church was considered to be a defilement of the church. Something that would ruin the Ohm.

So Deborah and I stopped having sex.

I applied myself to being a most excellent devotee. A disciple. I attended meetings. I ate cake. I lifted my face to the ceiling and sang emotional songs with tears streaming down my face. I was baptised. I learned to play the guitar. I learned to sing. I repeated people's names when they were introduced to me. I looked them in the eye. I did the two-handed handshake thing.

I spoke in tongues, an experience I can only describe as a kind of divine madness, a waking actionable meditation that voids the mind of any graspable thought until it resembles something like that rushing sky back in Dave's courtyard. I was in deep.

Now, I know you won't have seen this coming, but Deborah and I struggled hard not to have sex. We struggled and (you won't believe this) we failed. We failed often. Spectacularly. We oscillated between intense shame sessions and intense sex sessions. The forbidden nature of our 'failings' provided the act with an intensity that made it seem downright . . . well, spiritual. I experienced intense guilt and shame over this part of my life, a guilt and shame my young mind had not got around to developing on its own.

One afternoon my mother and I were driving to a netball game. It was a crystal-clear blue Sydney day. Elton John was on the radio. Mum had been reading Ian Roberts's biography in an effort to understand my being gay. Bless her, she was trying. 'Mum,' I said, 'what do think God thinks about me being gay?' She said nothing for a moment and then replied, 'Well, it's been hard for me to understand, but as long as you're a good person I think God would be okay with it. And if I want to keep my daughter in my life, I have to accept it.' She had brought herself a long way from the day she and my father cornered me in the kitchen and forced me to come out to them, then asked me to leave the house for a few days before insisting on family counselling to 'fix me'. This was real, proper progress.

'That's what you think,' I said, 'but what does *God* think?' She wasn't expecting that. Me? The headstrong, outspoken, unapologetically leftie gay of the family had found God? *And* denounced her gayness? Such a miracle was all the proof my mother needed.

I converted her, my father and my brother to the church. I had come out as an ex-gay.

I've always found revelation seductive. From a young age I was fascinated by folk tales, their meanings and our obsession with telling them. I loved that these stories had the magical ability to take things that seemed confusing or obtuse and render them in clear relief. Ah ha!

The Bible has a lot of 'Ah ha!' Its epic stories are filled with people being led by an unknowable force through chance meetings, long journeys and mistaken identities. Liars, thieves, scoundrels and underdogs alike. Kings, queens, orphans, magicians, and people who hear voices coming from burning trees. Sometimes the most important of them make only brief appearances before abruptly vanishing. And sometimes those who seem inconsequential at the start wind up as heroes. It's impossible to predict who will be what, but all of them are on their way to an 'Ah ha!'

At some point I became the leader of a youth group. I called my youth group The Filter Room. This was supposed to be just vague and confusing enough for people to impose their own meaning on it. I made month-long schedules of activities that I printed on A4 bits of orange paper, designed to be folded down and fit into teenagers' pockets without diminishing their aesthetic appeal. As if graphic design was the key to winning the souls of those under the age of eighteen.

We met in the community centre of a government housing complex in Surry Hills. The complex was famous for its oppressively high towers and its suicide rate. Each time we entered, we passed under a sign that said, 'Beware of falling TVs.' The place was filled with a musty-smelling collection of donated books in second-hand shelves. The woman who let us in each Friday was about sixty, with white hair and psoriasis skin. She was a resident in the complex who donated her time to making the centre available to people as much as her health, and the health of those she cared for, would allow. As she plugged her keys into the security door, I'd ask her how she was. Each and every time she responded, 'If I were any better, I'd be twins.'

The kids in the group were mostly the children of parents who had become saved. I didn't know much about their home lives or how they felt about having landed in this odd world of people speaking in tongues and falling down when preachers touched their foreheads. These kids seemed curious but also a bit dubious and, on that level, I connected with them. Somehow they had ended up in my charge for a few hours a week.

I was completely out of my depth. I was twenty years old, I was gay, I was saved, and I was trying my best to understand the Ohm as something that could be taught to others.

One of the boys in the group and I struck up a friendship. It was one of those friendships that develops slowly, as a result of unavoidable amounts of time spent together. Marc was about fourteen or fifteen. He was supremely confident, non-athletic and afflicted with a terrible case of hormonal acne, and he possessed that most desirable of human qualities: the ability to laugh at oneself.

I had an old yellow Ford Laser hatchback and I would pick him up from his house in Dulwich Hill or his school in Hurstville and drive him to our Friday night meetings and then I'd drive him home again.

These car rides became my lighthouse. I was lonely and still struggling with being gay in an environment that was contrarily both loving and hostile. We found we shared a love of movies and music. I'd drive him home and we would sit out the front of his house talking for long stretches. I learnt a lot from him. Without him I would never have discovered the album *Parachutes* by Coldplay, a brilliant bit of emotional indie-pop and an example of a band accidentally stumbling upon their best work first.

A lot of that time in the church I felt like a fake, but the time I spent with Marc I didn't feel like a fake at all.

I knew he looked up to me and I took that seriously. But I suspect neither of us considered that I might be looking up to him too.

One evening he told me he was being picked on at school by kids calling him gay. I felt my entire psyche stiffen. Was this a kid in my Pentecostal youth group coming out to me? Was he looking to me to tell him what to do? To be the voice of God? It was winter and it was raining. Inside my old car we were being enveloped by that old wet car smell. 'Well,' I ventured, 'do you think they're on to something?'

He thought about this very briefly. And then, with his signature vulnerability and confidence, he told me that he did not feel gay but he was worried that he might end up being convinced of his gayness by his peers because right now he didn't seem straight enough. This floored me. I told him that he should not let anyone tell him who he was. But I suspect he didn't need me to tell him that.

The Ohm was holding up a mirror.

Here was a boy whom the world was trying to convince was gay. Here was a girl, trying to be what she felt God wanted.

I left the church abruptly. I bought myself some time by telling the pastor I was going on an eight-week holiday but really I was going to my job each day and spending the evenings writing for hours. I was terrified that my fellow churchgoers would track me down, harass me, and convince me not to leave. After about six weeks, I wrote an emotional email to my pastor telling him I would not be returning to the church. I received a short acknowledgement. One day some people from the church came to my house but I was stoned and there was a woman they didn't know there. No one visited me again.

The second time I came out to my parents, we were in their living room. The house was completely silent as I explained to them that the American woman sharing my apartment was not my flatmate. I endured a painful speech from my dad about how doing what I knew was wrong in God's eyes would mean things would be much worse for me. I cried. But how could I blame my parents for trying to save me?

Deborah continued with church for a long while after I stopped. Sometimes I ran into her at family functions because she and my parents were at the same church, but we didn't speak much. I didn't see Marc again, though I thought of him often. And whenever I was in Surry Hills, I thought fondly about the psoriasis woman who would be twins if she were any better.

About a year after I left the church I was making dinner in the kitchen of my apartment in Maroubra. It was a cool evening and I could hear the ocean faintly over the sound of the humming range hood. I got a phone call. It was Marc. He had called to tell me that he had won the AFI Young Film Critics Competition, a nationwide contest. I was thrilled for him. He generously told me that so much of what he knew about film he'd learned in our conversations, and he asked me if I would I like to hear the review that had won him the competition. 'Yes! Of course!' I said. 'What film did you review?' '*Mulholland Drive*,' he said. That tickled me. Who in God's name wins a film critic competition reviewing *Mulholland Drive*? Marc. Marc Fennell does that.

I was suddenly standing in my kitchen, turning down the heat on some spattering mushrooms, listening to a boy I'd had such an intimate friendship with read me the most clear and comprehensible explanation of one of history's most incomprehensible films. I smiled broadly as he explained *Mulholland Drive* to me with ease and clarity, as if it was *Forrest Gump*. Each and every cell in my body was charged with a fuzzy, glittery joy. I was bursting with an important understanding of the universe that I couldn't quite put my finger on, like a dream on waking. I felt charged, rapturous. Affirmed. I slept peacefully in the bed I'd made that night.

And the Ohm, as it always does, went on.

Maxine Kauter

Maxine Kauter is a singer, songwriter and storyteller obsessed with all things language and narrative. She is best known for her role as the titular character in the long-running soap opera, *The Maxine Kauter Band*. In that role she has self-released three records of critically acclaimed music for sad sacks.

She is also the founder of *Museophilliac,* producing bespoke content and performances for cultural institutions. In that capacity she has written content and produced shows for The City of Sydney, The Australian Museum, the Royal Ontario Museum and various art and design galleries including the independent curatorial space The Cross Art Projects.

THE ANATOMY OF A FUCK BUDDY

David Cunningham

First delivered as a socioanthropological paper at the January 2018 plenary session of the prestigious Queerstories Society, Sydney's leading cultural research institute into the queer experience. Now published by gracious permission in this, the august transactions of this learned body.

PART 1: DEFINITIONS – FUCKS, BUDDIES, FUCK BUDDIES

To be, to have, a Fuck Buddy is a curious thing. It's a very different creature to enjoying a friend with benefits, in which the greatest benefit probably ought to be friendship; you would likely call a friend in an emergency, but almost certainly not a Fuck Buddy – unless it was a sexy emergency. Yet nor is it just the sum total of repeated one-night stands, for that would merely be a series of common or garden fucks. No, it's the 'buddy' part that's odd. A buddy – that glib and shallow word somewhere between acquaintance and friendship whose prime characteristic is providing the certainty of not being alone. A tennis buddy saves you from serving ball after ball into the distant nowhere. It's not even squash! A drinking buddy excuses an amount of alcohol that would be worrying if consumed alone. We raise our children by the buddy system: look at a primary school class, snaking out a gate safely in double file through the perils beyond the playground to the library or a public swimming pool or maybe even all the way to Questacon. When they venture forth, they do so holding hands, perhaps as friends, perhaps not, but definitely as buddies, that they might with greater assurance face the world together. Why, even in our very selves, when the ardent sperm meets the fecund egg, our chromosomes join hands along the double helix, buddies spinning together the thread of life itself.

So much for the buddy. Let us proceed to the fucks. What is sex? I have extensively reviewed the archival record, preferably in HD, and conducted practical fieldwork assaying my own body as the most proper object of study – a sort of wanking Montaigne. There have even been occasions, albeit infrequently, when volunteers saw the value of my research and joined me in my work. I have concluded that the necessary ingredients of sex may be described in the simple figure of the Fuck Triangle. Moisture. Friction. Warmth. All three must be present for sex to be good. If one corner of the Fuck Triangle should be missing, you're welcome to try, but according to Cunningham's Law of Fucks, you are unlikely to have a good time.

With our two core elements thus defined, let us attempt a synthesis. Humans are pattern-seeking animals, not least in the bedroom, and the desire to repeat a mutually satisfactory Fuck Triangle, and perhaps even hone it to greater perfection, is a deep-seated urge. To combine the fuck and the buddy, is to create, in theory, a profoundly humane institution. After all, it was only because Eleanor Roosevelt was hustled from the room that the United Nations Declaration of Human Rights did not enshrine an inalienable birthright to seek and share reliable fucks.

PART 2: FROM TRIANGLE TO PRISM – FUCKS AND LOVE

Pray recall again to your minds Cunningham's Fuck Triangle. How you arrange your Fuck Triangles is up to you. Some people are happy for theirs to be adjacent, congruent, tessellating like the trellised panes in the windows of a Tudor or Elizabethan house. Through these latticed Fuck Triangles, the light of physical pleasure with each successive partner shines pure and clear as pre-cum in the spring. Others – most? – certainly me, prefer to concentrate their triangles with just one person, fuck by fuck, laid one behind the other to build up a Fuck Prism. Of course, this prism also shines with that shimmering sensuous white light of pleasure given and received, of honest joy shared in lusty frenzy or languid comfort, of bodies meeting, melding with mutual enthusiasm, striving together towards the dazzling oblivion of orgasm. Of course. But align your fucks into a prism, and something else happens.

I base the following analysis on Sir Isaac Newton's ground-breaking book of 1704, called *RomantOpticks: or, a Treatise on the Refractions, Inflexions and Colours of Fucking*. It is a work at once visionary, acute and extremely horny.

Newton, himself single and almost certainly a virgin to the grave, nevertheless had the clarity to see that light passed through a prism does not emerge unchanged as through a window, however variegated its panes. No, through a prism, that first light of pure sex is refracted into its constituent parts, and fans out in the full spectrum of the rainbow, beaming an infinity of colours, of richness unimaginable when considering the white light that shone straight through that first, flat Fuck Triangle. And what are these many colours – a dreamcoat, if you please! – that combines commitment and compassion, humour and humility, sex and security? Well, the Emperor Constantine declared on the Milvian bridge that there is no palladium without a pal, but let us go further. What else is the rainbow standard around which we rally than, dare I say, that many-splendoured thing: love.

Love, as I have observed though not quite experienced, is a dynamic, changeable state. Of course, in the first flush of youth I imagined myself to be in love with the first viable crush of university days, not the forlorn hope of the schoolyard infatuation, which in the prudent discretion of the Sutherland Shire in the late 1990s could not be risked in open avowal. This was the real deal, a man with an ex-boyfriend (that proved it) and the self-assurance to live an uncloseted life true to himself. I'll spare you his name, but to me he was a vision beyond rational measurement; when he spoke, I was mesmerised by his tempting lips, which were naturally as red as the slightly chewy outer coating of a Monte Carlo's creamy payload. And the words those lips expressed in the face of my clumsy, furtive, almost imperceptible advances were as soft and sweet as the secret whiteness harboured in the heart of the Monte Carlo. And speaking eloquently to the untapped hormones of my chaste body was his own, firm and rugged all over like the strong biscuit shells of the Monte Carlo, which, as it transpires, is the hottest of the assorted creams.

The details of negotiating the boundaries between friendship, sex and potential love would require a lengthy appendix to properly convey and shall be omitted from this paper. Suffice it to say that he was my first, from kiss to full penetration in an hour. In my recently virginal naiveté, I imagined that one wonderful fuck, patient, kind, and above all, fun, was a pledge of a bright forever. It was not. He deftly sidestepped my alluring offers of microwave lasagna at the family home while Mum was away, and deflected my romantic limericks – the ideal verse form for misguided courtship within the iron 140-character limit of the text message, save perhaps the haiku. Ultimately, he took the time and courtesy to let me down gently, for which I remain very grateful. I have never since approached any nearer the courts of Venus than in that first disappointed foray, but the comparison I came to appreciate between the good honest sex of that first outing and the parade of fumblings from a succession of apps that rose, enjoyed a zenith of vogue then faded, was of empirical value (farewell gaydar.com.au, adieu manhunt.net, vale www. gay.com!). Fucks may be fun, but they are not fungible; no two are alike, even shared over and over with the same partner.

How fits this into our schema? Let us continue. On a long-enough timescale, the glass of our Fuck Prisms acts like a liquid. The soaring windows of a mediaeval cathedral are imperceptibly pooling at the bottom through the centuries; you may recall from your schooldays this phenomenon demonstrated with a viscous synthetic rubber in the Slow Flow exhibit on one of your long walks to Questacon. So too with the prism of loving mono-gamy, or more, though let's keep our prism in this discussion triangular for simplicity's sake; otherwise, the optics become very complicated indeed. It works, but alas I fear we have not the time within the narrow confines of this paper.

The Love Prism may or may not shatter under the impact of events; however, it is guaranteed to slowly change shape over time, so that every couple's rainbow will diverge from the simple fairytale of happily ever after. But the rainbow is richer for its hues being refracted in an admixture utterly unlike any other relationship, its colours in proportions that make each love unique and irreplaceable. If you prefer, think of it as tree rings for feelings. Right, that's enough holiday from all this prism shit! A metaphor pushed too far becomes a conceit, so let us press on and see how far we can get.

PART 3: THE FUCK BUDDY – A MIDDLE STATE?

(a) Establishment and equilibrium

Between the flat, two-dimensional windowpanes of casual sex through which light glitters with simple, some might say meretricious brilliance and the prism of romantic love steadily deepening into a third dimension – depth – we finally arrive at the middle state: the Fuck Buddy, amphibious between sex and love. The freedoms of the unalloyed Fuck Triangle mingled with the intimacy of the Love Prism. This was certainly the experience I enjoyed for some years with my Fuck Buddy, who I have no hesitation in naming Tom, for I never knew his real name.

Tom was a nom de plume that an outwardly diffident but improbably horny Thai man a few years my senior went by on manhunt.net, where he first approached me as a headless torso, like a sexy ghost. That golden body, projected flickering in pixelated promise from the immensity of the internet by cathode ray onto the screen and into my fancy, was a godsend. Insofar as Cleopatra is closer to us in time than she herself was to the construction of the Pyramids of Giza, so too was I far closer to virginity than to sexual maturity; indeed, I could count my experiences before Tom on one hand, when that hand was not otherwise employed in routine maintenance checks on my genital apparatus to ensure prime functioning should opportunity present itself. Tom was that opportunity. The clarity of what was on offer was hugely refreshing to someone more used to the tentative, half-voiced infatuations of a wasting youth. Tom was my El Dorado, my Prester John for whom I had long searched as saviour to fill my empty holes and heart against loneliness and inner whispers of every kind of inadequacy. In short, pending a first trial, Tom wanted to be Fuck Buddies.

He was my sexual education. He fucked – we fucked – well. By happy chance, we had the good fortune of sexual simpatico from the beginning. We soon settled into a routine that lasted over three years: just a simple text of 'Sleep yet?' was enough to set the wheels in motion at any hour up to four in the morning. I would drive the fifteen minutes across the bridge to his bedsit, three storeys up in a North Shore block of flats. His windows would be dark except for the light of the fibre-optic lamp on his sill. Its fronds waved gently and shifted colour in the night, an erotic anemone luring me into its tendrils with the caressed promise of 'No harm shall come to you' ('A lie! Jab jab jab with my stingers' – but more on that to come.) From the portraits of the Thai royal family on the wall, it became clear from inference, and then the partial intimacy of pre- and post-fuck pleasantries, that he was a graphic designer who in his spare time helped produce the expat community's loyalist newsletter. Part of our ritual, the comforting, predictable ruts we rutted into being, was for me to politely inquire after the health of His Majesty, the now former King Bhumibol the Great, otherwise Rama IX. He never asked after the Queen's health in return, but I generously overlooked that . . . for now.

The hybrid nature of the Fuck Buddy – single fucks fused one into another – however inadvertently, forms a bond that mirrors in many respects both the good and bad of a full-blown relationship. It is reliable, familiar, and therefore needs must become routine, even mundane. It became quite common for me to run little errands for Tom, like picking up fuck-groceries of amyl and lube on the way home – his home, naturally. Saddled with housemates, my bed remained a fortress of clean sheets. We sometimes pooled our respective toys to see what throwing a few more silicone mortices and tenons into the mix might achieve;

the tender-hearted among you might like to consider letting your dildos sleep inside your fleshlights for their mutual comfort!

I helped him shift a new mattress once, all the better to fuck on. Even though my attachment to the arrangement grew, the only outward relics we left were the spent condoms, the unusually verdant plant in his apartment building's foyer garden where I habitually spat water gargled from my bottle on departing, and of course the time-stamped electronic toll statements from crossing the Harbour Bridge at all hours, which I mercifully managed to keep Mum from seeing. For an enchanted two years all was well, and the light shone clear and comforting through the increasing depth of our Fuck Prism, deepening a mutual attachment and satisfaction.

(b) Deterioration, endgame and conclusions

Unlike the clear and even light refracted from a prism fused from love, there is a lurking imperfection in the prism made with a Fuck Buddy – at least for mine. Tom's and my arrangement came, imperceptibly at first, then with gathering speed, to partake of the compromise and frustrations of a fully fledged relationship. The glass of our Fuck Triangles had not the pellucid clarity of either fling or forever; it harboured blemishes, bubbles of ignorance that refracted the light from its true course into unsettling distortions. Over time the idiosyncrasies and asymmetries that lurked beneath our apparent sexual compatibility began to grate.

For my part, the forceful skull-fucking blowjobs he exacted when in full abandon to his lust had none of the thrill of submission, but rather the uncomfortable feeling of being a sink with a blockage being cleared by the meaty tool of a clumsy but enthusiastic plumber. Likewise, he wouldn't rim my fresh and wholesome bottom despite it being my favourite, even though my tongue traced the dizzy rounds of his anus like a twenty-cent piece racing down a money-spinner charity coin-vortex of the kind found in suburban shopping centres. Between Fuck Buddies, between Tom and I, the only real means of communication, of negotiation, argument and reconciliation, was our sex, which inevitably grew more freighted with implicit meaning as fucks and time added to the thickness and complexity of our shared prism. I was too young to communicate reservations with confidence, instead carrying on with outward gusto while disillusionment built quietly within, unshared and unaddressed.

While the repeated knowing of a Fuck Buddy provides a simulacrum of a relationship's intimacy, that intimacy may ultimately remain an illusion. At first intoxicated by that phantom amyl-addled mirage, then piqued by the curiosity of exploration, lulled by the complacency of comfort and finally bound by a sense of duty, I crossed boundaries with Tom I ought not to have. I was slowly coaxed by Tom and my own weaknesses towards the very real physical intimacy of frequent bareback sex. We both said we were the only one with whom the other enjoyed that mingling of cum and mucus in an ambrosial cocktail best admired, rather than drunk. But what assurance had we? Truth or lie, we had none. No orifice is a window to the soul. This was of course before PrEP, back when the only true prophylaxis was exposure to risk and shame.

The darkness of ignorance bred in me doubt – doubt about other men in the vast world of his life beyond that one bedroom where I knew him. Doubt that occluded the fair warm light of hearty, honest lust into something pale and wintry. Dim, feeble, faltering on my part were the refractions it cast through our Fuck Prism. Sunset deepened behind the darkening clouds of my mistrust and slowly passed into night. Haunted by the spectre of his dick reimagined as a death syringe, I broke it off, and the flawed, fragile prism we built together out of those crystal then clouded Fuck Triangles shattered, for me irrevocably.

The STI test afterwards revealed that both he and I had been telling the truth, and that the canker gnawing in my head and heart and butt had been of my own imagining, yet no less real for that. Given the abject failure of my kickstarter, there is no drone camouflaged in sequins that can surveil with impunity gays of interest into any nightclub. I have concluded that it all comes down to trust, at least for the present (please give generously).

You may be interested that, perhaps as fate's lesson for my misplaced bad faith, I did go on to contract a Byronic dose of syphilis – what they used to call being an incurable romantic. This despite the fact that, since Tom, I've never sexed without being scrupulously rubbered up to the armpits. I'm almost sure it was from the Fuck Nonagon of that lacklustre threesome: two tops, one versatile – if I'm the only hole in town, jump in, boys, the water's fine! The handful of non-infectious spirochetes swimming in my blood, the legacy of my doubts, will always be specks in my Fuck Triangles, but no longer a fault in the brittle glass of Fuck Buddies forsworn. I hope one day to share the joyous mutual project of forming a truly beautiful Fuck Prism with someone special, wherein those flaws will leave only the smallest ripples in the rainbow we shine forth together. Colleagues of this learned society, I would truly welcome your serious-minded collaboration in this important experiment, and any interested parties are directed to my correspondence address, listed on the relevant page of this volume.

David Cunningham

David Cunningham is a writer/researcher on ABC TV's *The Checkout*, who occasionally plays large men in top hats, togas and so on; apparently, it's cheaper than getting a proper actor. He was the runner up in the Raw National Stand-up Comedy Competition in 2008, and occasionally can be found doing stand-up around Sydney until it gets too much for his knees; he is therefore much more frequently found speaking from the big comfy chair at Story Club, stablemate of Queerstories at the Giant Dwarf theatre.

For leisure, he is in his ninth year of not-quite-failing a history PhD about ideological tensions in cultural representation of naval officers who were also members of parliament between the Glorious Revolution and the fall of the Walpole Ministry. Fellers, he's single!

A COUNTRY PRACTICE

Peter Taggart

This year I returned to my home town in south-west Queensland for what felt like the final time. After a two-year absence, I made the trip to pack up the family home and help my mother move to a new one in Brisbane. As could be expected, there were arguments and hot tears and the sense of an ending loomed large over each minor act. You cannot shy away from nostalgia when moving. There is memory in every object, on every trophy shelf and at the back of every cupboard. I tried to shield myself from some of it, creating distraction with podcasts and music, but it was a futile exercise and the Blu-Tacked reminders of awkward teen years torn from bedroom walls would only re-emerge, pieced together and laid bare, in those quietest hours of night.

St George is about 500 kilometres south-west of Brisbane, a dusty trek down the Moonie Highway to a country of cotton farms and cattle. The lifeline of the district is the mighty Balonne River, which rivals the Brisbane River in all its muddy-brown glory and eagerness to flood. The community itself is known for raising rugby league players, the occasional politician and even more occasionally, pescatarian homosexuals with failing eyesight. I spent my first seventeen years there, riding my pushbike on the outskirts of town, dodging swooping magpies and daydreaming about what my life might be like in a place big enough to have its own McDonald's.

As is so often the case, my classmates seemed to be aware I was different before I was. Though I never recognised it as bullying, they took a particular joy in pointing out any trace of a lisp or the flamboyant way I gestured when I spoke. If anyone was direct enough to call me a faggot, I would always respond, 'You know, a faggot is actually a bundle of sticks' – which is not just the perfect answer of a faggot, but of a huge nerd as well.

Before you get too worried, this is not a story of heroism in which I tell you how I overcame issues of identity to not just survive, but flourish in outback Queensland, nor is it a story of how my shining example inspired old friends and neighbours to vote in favour of marriage equality – it didn't, and the electorate of Maranoa returned among the highest majorities of 'No' votes in the country. Rather, this is simply the heartwarming story of a heterosexual wasteland and a closeted teenager desperately hunting for porn.

In the early noughties the gayest thing a man ever did in St George was sit down to urinate. Masculinity was the ultimate prize, bootcut was the only acceptable variety of jean and

Brokeback Mountain had not yet been released, ruining the Sherpa trucker jacket for everyone. Federal Member for Kennedy, Bob Katter, once claimed he'd walk 'backwards from Bourke' if there was anything resembling a gay community in his far north Queensland seat. It wasn't an entirely surprising thing to hear. Gay folk in regional areas exist, but prove fairly easy to ignore should you have the willpower. St George didn't really have a large number of gay people when I was there and those who did choose to live in town were the subject of cruel gossip and derision. It meant they kept themselves, and their relationships, discreet, if not entirely hidden. Living any other way was to tempt fate.

Growing up in a small country town was to grow up in a homosexuality vacuum of sorts. I was aware of gay people – I saw them being routinely mocked on *The Footy Show* – but aside from being a punchline they were presented as a sort-of neutered people, deprived of their own sexual agency. I found it difficult to picture them having active sex lives and whenever I did try and imagine what two men could conceivably do with each other, it was akin to torture. I was totally clueless. I recall one head-scratching moment when I was a fourteen year old on school camp. Finishing another grim meal in the rec hall one evening, a friend returned to my table with two bowls of dessert. She held up the steaming sticky date pudding and gleefully said, 'You know what they call sticky date, don't you? Poofter pie!' We both laughed and ate, before going on our merry way. But I returned to my dorm that night deeply confused. 'But how does that work?' I thought. 'Why would it

be called that? Where's the "pie"? And what's sticky, and how?'
I mulled over this for months, like it was not a dirty joke but
a brilliant maths equation and I was the gay version of Russell
Crowe in *A Beautiful Mind*.

I couldn't turn to any of our reliable institutions for answers,
because as far as 'the talk' went, gay sex didn't happen. Sure,
we were taught the mechanics of reproductive sex in the senior
years of primary school, but at eleven years old I already had
a pretty good handle on what went on there – a married man
would put his entirely flaccid penis inside his wife's vagina,
which, to my understanding, sat just below the belly button
and was a perfectly round circle, as if drawn with a compass
and HB pencil. Unlike my best friend, I did not go on to study
medicine.

If gay sex ever was mentioned, it was always presented as a
horrifying act, and the invention of a defective mind. Everyone
I heard speak of it, be they child or adult, would express their
shock and repulsion that a grown man could want to put his
penis . . . up there. The anus was a sacred space, perhaps even
a huge secret, and was spoken of in such hushed, reverential
tones that the first time I saw one up close I expected people to
be praying inside of it. It was high and mighty talk for a town
where one of the most popular forms of contraception was 'up
the bum, no babies'. And while the act itself did sound mighty
disgusting when other people described it, I was at least wise
enough to understand that disgusting and morally reprehens-
ible are two very different things. Besides, I knew there were
plenty of obscene by-products of heterosexual sex too – thrush,

urinary tract infections, and perhaps the most heinous, the creation of human life.

Before I could fully come to terms with my sexuality, I needed to satisfy my curiosity and find out whether I truly wanted what my idiotic pubescent mind was telling me I wanted. I needed to see a grown adult man who didn't look like Barnaby Joyce or Joh Bjelke-Petersen. I had to observe gay sex in all its messy, sweaty joy, removed from the judgement of the Sunday prayer set. I wanted some awareness of the uncharted waters I was in before wading any deeper. In a town like St George, however, it would be a wild scavenger hunt for clues and I'd have to explore the old-fashioned way – through magazines and television and possibly the microfiche at the local public library.

Finding pornography is not as easy as they'd have you believe in the movies. If you were a gay youth in the early noughties you didn't inherit a big box of X-rated DVDs from your friend's older brother, nor could you find a stack of back issues of soft-core *DNA Magazine* underneath the local Magic Faraway Tree. My ready access to straight pornography was perhaps the cruellest irony. From the age of fourteen I worked behind the counter at the local newsagent and I'm not sure many people know this, but most old magazines don't get returned to their publisher. I hope I'm not blowing this story wide open, but if a magazine fails to sell, the newsagent just rips off the cover for return and the bulk of the magazine gets dumped out the back of the shop. So behind my local newsagent there was a huge trailer filled with *That's Life* and *Take 5*, yes, but also *Ralph* and *Penthouse* and *Playboy*. It was quite the treasure trove, but slim pickings if you were more interested in Chad Michael Murray than Carmen Electra. This was the early noughties, as I've mentioned.

Occasionally, you could find a man's bare arse in *Black+White* magazine, but as we all know *Black+White* was simply an arts publication and *not* pornography. A rare trailer find would be a discarded copy of *The Australian Naturist* magazine, which was exactly what it sounds like. *The Naturist*'s core mission was seemingly to strip all the sexuality out of being nude and only really appealed if you had a particular kink for blurry shots of fat granddads playing tennis.

Aside from *The Naturist*, there was but one publication reliably publishing full-frontal photos of men. That's right, I'm talking about *The Picture* magazine's 'Home Blokes'. 'Home Blokes' was a regular one-page feature in the weekly magazine and was a pre-Tinder outlet where straight men could send pictures of their dicks. Knowing no heterosexual woman in her right mind would touch a copy of *The Picture*, this was essentially straight men throwing a bone – sometimes literally – to gay men. But before we honour these brave pioneers for their act of charity, it's important to note that 'Home Blokes' was so revolting it might have been a sly form of gay conversion therapy.

Firstly, imagine the type of straight reader who would send in a photo of himself to *The Picture* magazine. Then imagine the most tortured-looking penises that could still reasonably be expected to hang from a human body. These weren't so much dicks as they were blood-engorged props from the set of *Mad Max: Fury Road*. If you're unfamiliar with 'Home Blokes', trying to be turned on by it is the equivalent of getting home from a big night out and facing off against a dusty can of cream of asparagus soup at the back of your pantry – you don't have a taste for it, you certainly don't want it, but if you don't eat it – you'll starve.

It was after the 'Home Blokes' discovery that I first got a TV in my room – a pivotal moment in the life of any adolescent. Bought using my own hard-earned newsagent wage, the television was the size of a lunch box and produced crystal clear black and white images whenever the antenna felt like it. A TV of one's own afforded a liberation I hadn't had previously and suddenly I too was free to roam late night SBS, looking for men from the Eastern Bloc caught with their pants down.

It's a very common story that men around my age would secretly watch the US version of *Queer as Folk*, which filled the sought-after time slot of 10 pm on Monday night. I would watch with a blanket over the TV to obscure the glare and the sound completely muted, which was fine because I wasn't tuning in for the stellar dialogue. It was an eye-opening experience week after week, watching Brian and Justin and Ted navigate the world of gay dating and exhilarating Pittsburgh night-life. I'd patiently sit through every episode waiting for someone to hook up. It was a deeply rewarding exercise. I'll never forget watching Emmett get fucked in an aeroplane bathroom by his elderly partner – who then promptly died of a heart attack while still inside him – and thinking 'Look at all the wonderful possibilities the future holds!'

It was a great moment of anxiety when *Queer as Folk* eventually finished up. It would not just leave a void in my Monday night viewing schedule, but a gap in my knowledge of gay life. I needn't have worried, though, for as soon as *Queer as Folk* disappeared, it was replaced by a show I found a lot sexier – HBO's prestige prison drama *Oz*. Is it deeply problematic to have a sexual awakening while watching a violent TV show set inside a maximum-security penitentiary? Possibly. Did I find one of the white supremacist gang members pretty hot? Yes, but it doesn't mean I'd vote for him. Did I immediately recognise the show's Catholic nun as Rita Moreno from *West Side Story*? Of course I did, and she was excellent.

I hate to say this, but as a questioning teenager, seeing Christopher Meloni's convict penis on TV once a week wasn't really cutting it. Getting reasonable internet access at home was a real game changer and by reasonable, I mean country reasonable. A low-res jpeg would take thirty seconds to load and if you wanted to download a ten-minute video, it could take up to three days. So if you wanted to watch something on, say, a Saturday evening, you'd really have to get organised around Wednesday morning. This type of planning ahead has produced a generation of incredibly organised and ultimately very employable queer millennials.

I was, of course, completely terrified by the prospect of Mum or Dad ever coming across a gay video or image, so I, like many teens of the era, became an expert at clearing search history and deleting cookies. Fearing I'd not been as vigilant as I'd thought, I hatched a plan to really throw them off the scent. I decided to download some images of hardcore straight pornography, and in a normal move, print them out and assemble them as part of a gorgeous scrapbook. I would keep this scrapbook in a drawer in my bedroom and wait for it to be discovered by a curious parent, whose only response would be immeasurable relief. 'Thank God!' I imagined Mum saying, clutching the scrapbook to her chest. 'My heterosexual son has printed out a dozen very graphic pictures of a woman making passionate love to herself . . . and look, he's laminated them.'

When I say 'scrapbook', I hope you are not envisioning some hastily prepared, poorly conceived teenage interpretation of a hardcore 'girly mag'. Let me be clear, there was no 'scrap'. This was carefully curated and artfully executed. This was Anna Wintour preparing the September issue of *Vogue*. A good deal of thought went into the diversity of content – 'I already have an image of a woman getting head on page five – I *do not* need to see that on page seven.' I even went to great lengths to ensure a variety of women were represented, from the big-breasted to the frankly enormously breasted. The images, not unlike the models depicted, were neatly spread and the pages were tucked inside a blue display folder, awaiting their public debut.

Sadly, the scrapbook was never to be picked up. I'd vastly overestimated both my parents' interest in my private affairs and their willingness to clean my room. Abandoning all hope, I disposed of it years later. I know it probably ended up beneath a layer of apple cores and shattered beer bottles at the local tip, but I like to think it somehow ended up in the hands of a filthy magazine connoisseur or, in my wildest dreams, sitting among old copies of *House & Garden* on the coffee table of a doctor's waiting room.

When it came time to leave St George for university, I found myself putting a lot of pressure on Brisbane. I expected the simple act of moving to the city at seventeen to change my life in innumerable, impossibly beautiful ways. It's true there were pubs and clubs and better-stocked shelves of magazines, but the internet was as sluggish as ever. There were more gay people, certainly, but there were also more people to shout things at me from passing cars. I was once told, 'Go home, poofter!' and at the time I was standing across the road from my house. 'Sir,' I thought, 'please be patient.'

While I still felt like I had a lot of catching up to do, I soon shrugged off the burden of understanding all facets of gay life and started living one on my own terms. I forgave myself for each bizarre, hormone-fuelled episode and recognised I'd done my best, with what I had. I'd prepared a new chapter, in a place where previously I couldn't even turn the page. I had created something from nothing. I'd made lemonade out of lemons and a faggot out of a bundle sticks.

Peter Taggart

Peter Taggart is a writer and podcaster from Brisbane. He was born on the glittering Gold Coast and raised in St George – a small farming township in southern Queensland. In a painfully ordinary childhood, he didn't play with corn-husk dolls, nor did he ride around on his family's billion-acre property on a shiny BMX. Instead, he sat inside on hot summer days, eating TeeVee snacks and watching *Fast Forward* and seventies sitcoms.

Peter has written for *Junkee*, *The Guardian*, *Meanjin* and *SBS*, has hosted shows on 2SER/Star Observer Digital and 4ZzZ and has contributed to various programs on triple j and ABC Radio Brisbane. His podcasts include the popular *Bring a Plate* and less popular *Clip Show*.

A CLOCKWORK LEMON

Rebecca Shaw

My name is Rebecca Shaw, and I am a queer. This is not how I start every story I write, but in this case it is important. The thing I love most about 'Queerstories' is that it really showcases just how diverse and different our community is, no matter how much society wants to put us in boxes, or try to weigh us down with stereotypes that often aren't even true. Except for the stereotype that lesbians in their thirties named Rebecca are universally adored. That one is extremely true.

It's so amazing to hear stories from our collective histories, of paths taken, of struggles overcome – and it's nice to think about the next generation, having hope that there will be fewer stories of 'overcoming'. When I was a young girl growing up in Toowoomba in regional Queensland, I had to overcome a lot. First was my terrible personality. Then my extremely terrible haircut, which was actually only overcome about a year ago.

Besides those however, was the fact that every single day I was struggling against my sexuality and myself. I would push those feelings away, and wish that I were normal. Well, as normal as an extremely weird child whose favourite game was pretending to be a statue could be. I used to knock on the front door and when my mum would answer it I would freeze and say through clenched lips, 'I'm a statue'. I was a creative genius from early on, obviously.

I used to spend a lot of time wishing more than anything that I would wake up one morning and the crush I had on my brother's girlfriend who smelled like patchouli would be replaced with a crush on a boy at school. That the interest I pretended to have in Scott Wolf from *Party of Five* would be real, and not just something I talked about to keep up the pretense while I thought lesbian thoughts about Neve Campbell from *Party of Five*. That my love for Taylor Hanson wouldn't be because for a couple of months I thought he was actually a girl.

I would look at my female friends falling for and dating boys throughout high school, and I would wish I could be like them. Wish that, like one of my friends, *I* would be lucky enough to want to lose my virginity in a gross Gold Coast hotel room to a sloppily drunk guy on Schoolies week while 'Mambo No. 5' played in the background on repeat. Obviously those wishes never came true, and happily I ended up getting through that mindset, and coming out the other side never having had sex while 'Mambo No. 5' played in the background. Yet.

I have now evolved, like an extremely gay Pokémon, to see the real truth. I now realise how *truly* misguided I was back then. Partly because ideally it should have felt okay for me to be myself, but mainly because I now know that straight women do not deserve my envy.

They deserve my pity.

Now, obviously this does not apply to everyone – #notall-straightpeople – but I do believe that for a lot of women, terminal heterosexuality is to their detriment. Let's look at the facts. Number one – they only get to date men. Number two – they don't get to date women. These seem like similar facts, but it is an important distinction. Not only can you *only date men*, you also do not get the pleasure of dating women. It is a classic lose/lose situation, or a much sadder version of *Sophie's Choice*.

Don't get me wrong, some of my favourite people in the world are heterosexual women. That is exactly why this issue is *so* important to me. As someone who exists in the world, I am extremely familiar with how terrible a lot of straight cis men can be. But, as a lesbian, I have the privilege of largely being able to choose to avoid them outside of work and public spaces, using a system of complex underground tunnels via the sewerage system. This sounds disgusting but is still preferable to encountering groups of drunk straight men on the street at 11 pm in Newtown. It is very difficult for me to hear the harrowing tales from my straight female friends about trying to open thousands of terrible men chocolate bars in order to find the rare worthwhile straight man golden ticket hidden inside. And so I have found my calling as a sort of lesbian Willy Wonka, hoping to change their lives.

As a lesbian who doesn't pickle vegetables or play soccer, I have decided it's time to use my spare time to instead offer these women my assistance. I have written a pitch to apply for funding to create a retreat for heterosexual women, where they will undergo a scientific program I have developed with the help of no scientists at all in order to attempt to 'queer them up'. But *unlike* ex-gay therapies, where someone tries to turn another person heterosexual and take away ALL of their gay thoughts (such as 'When is the sequel to *Carol*?' or 'Did I, a human woman, just cough up a furball?'), our therapy is not taking away any choices. We do not want to destroy women's attraction to men; we are simply attempting to *add* queerness. It's like if dating a man is normal water, then dating NOT a man is like soda water, which is better, but dating women is like adding in tequila and lime to the soda water: now you've got a party. The option for women to still be attracted to and want to date men will *still be there* – it's just our firm belief that they will not *want to*, given the slightest chance at all.

The pitch first discusses recruitment: our recruitment will focus on heterosexual women who most closely fit the parameters defined by the principle of 'straight 5/queer 10'. If you haven't heard of straight 5/queer 10, it is the concept that some people who subvert or lie outside of the wider societal norms of what is attractive in the conventional straight world might be seen as more attractive in the queer world.

As a fat woman, if I had to appeal to straight men, I would be ranked as a negative 10 million according to male Facebook commenters on the articles I write. Luckily, I get to date people in the queer community who more often appreciate diversity of looks, such as women named Rebecca who wear graphic

T-shirts and jeans 100 per cent of the time. We all know straight women like this; those who go largely unappreciated by men for whatever reason, but who we all know would be in high demand with queer women. You can spot them easily in the wild – they are usually wearing a cardigan.

The pitch then focuses on some of what the program will cover. First comes the physical embodiment class – it is important for the heterosexual women to understand the scope of what is desirable to other women. This obviously can include dresses and high heels and make-up, but they are encouraged to try on other clothes that may not have previously appealed to most men, but will attract plenty of queer women. In a display that I imagine will feature as a fun dressing room montage in the film made about this successful program and my life, the attendees will try on an array of hats, boots, singlets, black shirts and denim jackets. And denim jeans. And denim literally every other item of clothing. There will also be a dedicated denim room that only plays Dannii Minogue songs, but she will be called Denim Minogue in order to keep on theme.

Women who wish to undergo the full authentic experience will also be given an asymmetrical haircut and septum piercing, but this is not mandatory.

Then comes the session that will be called either 'A Clockwork Lemon' or 'Clockwork Orange is the New Black'. This is where the women will watch hours of nonstop footage of happy queer women and couples, purring cats, Ellen dancing, GIFs of Gillian Anderson, and the good parts of *The L Word* (so after Jenny dies). And, of course, the final session is the one where a scientist or academic comes in and shows everyone the studies and research on how many more orgasms women have when sleeping with other women instead of with men.

I hope the pitch will be successful so we can start helping women Australia-wide, but worst case scenario, even if it doesn't work, they will all get a nice break from men while on the retreat.

You're welcome.

Rebecca Shaw

Rebecca Shaw (aka **@brocklesnitch**) is a writer and creator of popular parody Twitter account **@notofeminism**, which was developed into an illustrated book with Affirm Press.

She is on the writing team at *Tonightly with Tom Ballard*, and has written for *Junkee*, *The Guardian*, *Daily Life*, *Kill Your Darlings*, *SBS Comedy* and more. She is in constant competition with Ruby Rose to become Australia's favourite lesbian.

KEROUACKING OFF

Ben McLeay

Because I am not smart enough to imagine bad things happening to me, in the middle of 2017 I decided to drive 25 000 kilometres across America, alone, in a piece of shit 2000-model Ford E150 cargo van that I bought off a stranger for two thousand dollars. It went pretty well. A few times I nearly got stuck and only just narrowly avoided dying alone in the wilderness like the *Into the Wild* guy. I had a lot of what I would politely refer to as 'stomach problems' thanks to an ongoing disagreement with high-fructose corn syrup. At one point, I nearly had a car accident because two drunk hitchhikers had a fight in my car and one of them pulled the keys out of the ignition, locking the steering as I was driving around a corner at 70 miles an hour in a thunderstorm. But, despite these misadventures, my lack of imagination proved to be accurate: nothing bad happened to me. If anything, the diarrhoea made me look a little more svelte.

I saved every penny I earned working for years in a web development job that I hated because the only thing that makes me truly happy is driving by myself for long stretches at a time through new places. I'm not one of those #wanderlust people whose passion is taking staged 'candid' photos of themselves standing underneath waterfalls on Vietnamese beaches while drinking a discouragingly textured vegetable smoothie and wearing a big floppy hat. I am perfectly happy driving through somewhere completely uninteresting like, say, Kansas. I just don't want to be around people or places I know.

I am a very socially anxious person and the thought of getting to explore somewhere new without having to talk to anyone or accommodate anyone else's needs or expectations makes me practically vibrate with ecstasy. Waking up every day and being able to pick a random point on a map and drive to it without a care in the world is my idea of heaven. All in all, it was bliss.

When I told friends I would be doing this by myself for three months, a few of them seemed somewhat surprised. Some asked if I was worried about being shot. Frankly, I was not. While the US certainly has a problem with gun violence, most of it is directed either from police officers towards people of colour or from radicalised teens towards high schools, not from rednecks towards effeminate itinerant nerds with haircuts that make them look something like an extra in *Mad Max*.

I just couldn't imagine it happening. An Australian woman was shot by police in Minneapolis after she herself made the 911 call that summoned them, just two weeks prior to my arrival in the States, and there was still not enough juice in my brain to conjure up an image of something similar happening to me.

There were a few times I felt uncomfortable, but after a while you realise that every campground in America is littered with spent shotgun shells, not just the one you are staying in, and that, actually, the sound of gunfire is nothing to be overly concerned about. Apparently.

For all that we make fun of Americans for the insane way they have chosen to live their lives in a ridiculous hell of their own making, people in America tend to be, well, people. I believe people are generally good. We might for the most part be self-involved and kind of stand-offish, but on the whole we all want to help out the people around us where we can. We like being nice. It's fun.

Whenever I needed help, people offered it. On the rare occasions that I wanted company, people were happy to have a chat. At one campground, a couple invited me into their bus-sized RV to use their kitchen because they could see from their raised viewpoint that I was heating up soup inside my van on my little butane stove because it was snowing too heavily for me to cook outside. Another time, a single mum travelling alone set up her tent in the site next to mine in an otherwise entirely empty campground because she had never camped before and wanted someone nearby in case she was attacked by a bear. As a thank you, she brought a bottle of bourbon and a joint over to my campfire and we got so drunk that when I woke up the next morning to find a note that said 'Thank you for an incredible night', I had to madly try and remember if we had slept together or not. (We had not.)

Far from being violently hounded out of small town America in a fashion similar to that depicted in the documentaries *Rambo* or *Deliverance*, I drove in a big squiggly loop through a total of thirty American states and two Canadian provinces, collecting nothing but positive memories and VHS tapes. (This will come up later.)

One experience did shake me, though: crossing the border into Canada. Here I would like to, as they say, 'check my privilege'. I am a white dude from a Western country, so when I say that I had a bad experience, I don't mean that I was indefinitely detained or deported or separated from my family; I mean that someone was rude to me.

Since I was driving across the top of America already and didn't really have any itinerary to speak of, I figured I might as well dip a finger or two into Canada, driving over the border into Vancouver from Seattle. This left me in something of a pickle: Washington is one of the rare, majestic American states with legal weed, and I had bought a lot of it. I was absolutely enamoured by the idea of being able to choose a variety of products and strains from a person who knew what they were talking about, instead of giving fifty dollars to a friend of a friend of a friend and hoping that whatever I got was at least psychoactive to some degree and not just a few buds of marjoram. I spent the days prior to crossing the border trying to balance how good I was at hiding things in a van versus the terrible consequences of being caught versus how much money

I had spent on the weed I had (again, it was a lot). This might sound like something that only an idiot would consider and I can only say: yes.

Ultimately, I managed to look beyond my insane lust for drugs and I made the correct decision; I pulled off the highway and threw it all in a bin in a parking lot outside a supermarket just shy of the border.

This turned out to be very prudent, as, would you believe it, if you are a dishevelled young foreigner in a windowless van that is registered under a name that is not yours, the dutiful men and women of the Canada Border Services Agency are not going to wave you through without scrutiny. After a few brief questions accompanied by some raised eyebrows, I was directed to pull out of the queue by a lady that I bafflingly thanked profusely, because I am the softest man alive.

I was fully aware that border security and customs agents are, traditionally, not particularly lovely people in the pursuit of their work. They racially profile people, and they deliberately try to make you upset or uncomfortable in the hopes that you will slip up. They are paid to be dicks. Despite knowing this, I have to admit I expected Canadian border security to be a man in a Mountie uniform riding a moose bareback, whose sole job was directing me to the nearest Tim Hortons.

This was not the case.

I was shunted into a building where a man who looked like a disconcertingly hot version of Sean Spicer instantly began trying to trick me into admitting that I was smuggling both firearms and narcotics into the country. Admittedly, that was almost partially true until I came to my senses. Because I am a genius, I decided the best strategic response to his interrogation was to tell him an easily disprovable lie. I told Hot Sean Spicer unconvincingly that I hadn't been doing any paid work while over here and when he told me that it's actually legal to do so and there's no reason for me to lie, I was so incensed at the quite accurate accusation that I was lying that I lied again, insisting that I hadn't. I am basically the Garry Kasparov of conducting border security interviews.

Put off by my initial attempt at subterfuge, when asked if I had had any weed while in the marijuana-friendly state of Washington, I decided to be honest. I told him, yes, very much so; in fact I had a whole bunch with me until I binned it twenty minutes earlier. This did not please the man. How could I be so irresponsible? What if a bunch of bin-diving children found my stash of THC-infused gummies, he asked? And, true, that would be a terrible thing to have on my conscience. The thought of a bunch of teens getting stuck on the couch watching YouTube videos of how rubber bands are made for hours at a time shakes me to my very core. I carry the guilt of this irresponsible disposal with me to this day. In my defence, I offered that I did not know what else I was supposed to have done with them; he suggested I should have flushed them down the toilet; I countered that I don't think you're meant to flush rubbish down the toilet. As in a debate between two evenly matched intellectual giants, we were at an impasse.

Hot Sean Spicer proceeded to try to convince me that I was high. As a very impressionable person, this almost worked.

'Why are you so nervous? Why are your eyes so red?' For a second, I thought he was right, despite knowing full well I hadn't actually had any weed for about a week. 'I'm nervous because this is terrifying,' I told him. 'And my eyes are red because my entire body is extremely sensitive.' Unconvinced, he informed me that I got high so that I wouldn't appear nervous when traversing the border, a thesis which seemed instantly disprovable, given that I was at that time nervous as all fuck.

Seemingly satisfied, he moved on, asking for my keys and my phone. Casually, with the air of someone asking if the weather is nice, he asked for my passcode. I felt it then, a stirring to become one of those libertarians who film videos of themselves yelling at cops that they know their rights. But I also felt another thing, namely the desire not to get thrown into a lightless cell for forty-eight hours. Rightfully feeling like a complete dipshit, I told him. 'It's 420666.'

As we both silently acknowledged that I am not a genius, I was told to sit down and wait. Which I did, passing the time by coming to the realisation that the last thing I posted on Facebook was a piece with a caption that explicitly stated that I was paid by my job to write this, while overseas, about things I had been doing overseas.

For nearly half an hour, I was left staring at the wall with the terrified eyes of someone viewing a distant mushroom cloud, furiously attempting to concoct a further web of lies with which I could mitigate the flimsy web I had already constructed. I was saved from this nightmare of hypotheticals by further probing about my drug history which I, again, decided to respond to honestly. I was gently surprised to discover that you will not appear less suspicious if you tell them the amount of drugs you have done is 'heaps'.

After having every reflective surface on my person swabbed for cocaine and heroin, I was directed once more to sit down and be terrorised by my own thoughts. After marinating in panic for a while, I was summoned back to the counter. 'Okay, now we're suspicious,' the hot man said. Briefly, I experienced a moment of confused delight at the realisation that they had not been previously. 'Why do you have suitcases full of VHS tapes in your van?' Honestly, a great question. I could not reasonably explain to you right now why I collect VHS tapes, and I've had months to think about it, so you can imagine that my on-the-spot explanation to someone who had the power to ruin my life was not entirely convincing. Again, I was told to sit down and mull over all the dickhead decisions I had ever made in my life that led me to this point.

Then, abruptly, without explanation or apology, I was given my keys and phone and told that I could go. I was furious. I had spent a good hour thinking that my life was about to be ruined forever (the fact that I had committed no crime notwithstanding) as these people had attempted to bully me into slipping up, only to have the fact that I had done nothing wrong go completely unacknowledged. It was a trivial thing to fixate on, but I did – I spent the next few weeks reimagining the conversations I had with that awful, beautiful man, but this time I had perfect little burns for all of his questions. Hell, I still find myself doing it occasionally. In my mind, I fired a perfect parting shot as I left the building, reducing him to a tiny little bureaucratic worm. In reality, I crumpled like an origami unicorn in the rain and practically bowed to the man as I left.

I put off going back through US border control for days because I was so nervous about going through the same experience again, but this time with someone much more likely to shoot me with an AR-15 if they didn't like my tone of voice. Perversely, the border crossing from Alberta to Montana was almost comically pleasant. It was just one booth on a single-lane road, overlooking Glacier National Park. There was even a herd of buffalo grazing nearby – it could not have been more cartoonishly the opposite of what I had expected. My interrogation at the hands of this bizarrely friendly man amounted to him asking if I had any guns; when I said 'no', he waved me through and wished me a nice day.

If there was a lesson to be learned here I think it's that I was at least partially vindicated for my complete lack of imagination. For that hour or so, I took a brief foray into the world of speculating about the worst things that could happen to me, and not only was it horrible, it was also completely pointless. I lied to a federal officer after having barely avoided committing a serious federal crime on a whim, and absolutely nothing terrible happened to me. I will be fully vindicated when I die of something completely unexpected like getting hit by a meteorite, proving that it was pointless to have been worrying about anything else.

Ben McLeay

Ben McLeay is a Brisbane-based writer at Pedestrian.tv and co-host of political comedy podcast *Boonta Vista Socialist Club*.

He does roughly 10,000 tweets a day at **@thomas_violence** and would do just about anything for a free lunch.

BELONGING

Candy Royalle

Stepping off the plane, walking through the airport, the smell that hits is like many developing countries I've visited – dense, rich, unsterilised – recalling thoughts of exotic holidays. This time, I'm surrounded by people talking in a tongue I'm very familiar with. I can understand it and feel it; however, using it is a constant struggle that requires summoning childhood memories of faltering conversations with my grandmother. Both my parents decided they wouldn't speak to my brother and me in Lebanese; they didn't want us to experience the racism they had. Of course, this didn't protect us from the racist tongues of white people, and instead robbed us of a second language.

Walking through customs and being spoken to in Lebanese, I am still trying to gather the words required to answer the border inspector's questions when in flawless English he asks me the reason for my visit.

'I'm on holidays.'

'Is this your first time to Lebanon?'

'Yes.'

'But you're a Malouf?'

'Yes, I am.'

I've always existed somewhere in between. Between cultures and colours, genders and sexuality. Between spiritual and atheist, creator and imitator. Belonging had always been a theoretical idea for me, not a sensation rooted firmly in any place or person, any community or group.

For as long as I can remember, I have felt the call of Lebanon in my gut. Since the smell of my dad's lentil dish *mjardra* wafted through the house, since the painful, haunting and powerful voice of Fairuz played on the stereo, since my mother beckoned me into the kitchen and asked me to pour more olive oil over the tabouli while she mixed it with her hands, to taste it and tell her whether it needed more salt. Growing up in the bush, gum trees, red-bellied black snakes and hairy huge huntsmen felt as natural to me as picking parsley, trying to decipher Arabic when my parents were talking in secret or watching my aunties laugh as they belly danced to terrible nineties pop music. Those many worlds always felt like they fit together – the right sort of synergy. Still, I didn't feel like I fully belonged. My family would talk of traditional things that seemed archaic: the path a life should take; the sacrifices one had to make in order to adhere to the codes of a culture that was a big part of me, just not all of me. I was exposed to worlds outside the traditional that created conflicting ideas of existence.

At school, nothing felt right. There were boys whose affections were limited to sleazy come-ons and reasons why we should get busy in the out-of-bounds area. I was more interested in my latest girl crush. Most of the teachers didn't understand that I wasn't stupid, I just wasn't engaged. They'd made their minds up about me (and many of my Lebanese, Greek, Maltese and Italian friends) early on. I almost flunked my HSC completely but Dad, who was determined I was going to be a lawyer, made sure I went straight on to a night bridging course at Sydney University.

Sydney Uni happens to be right next to the infamous lesbian strip of King Street, Newtown. It was on King Street one evening after class that I stumbled upon one of the most popular dyke bars in Sydney. Back then, the Bank Hotel was dark and grimy and butch dykes would bring their own pool cues. I was introduced to a whole other world, one that I had spent my teens fantasising about. Out went night classes (and law altogether), in came rendezvous with women who taught me the ropes and showed me what lesbian Sydney looked like. It felt good, like I had almost made it home. Almost. But there weren't that many like me, and I didn't know how to find them. It was extremely rare in the late nineties and early noughties to meet any queers of colour in those spaces, so I started to believe I was always going to exist in some sort of periphery, where there were very few people like me.

Time passed, I moved through so many different types of me. The corporate me – before my full-blown social awakening – the artist me, the traveller me, the activist me. Every time I entered these new worlds, I found brimming communities, yet still felt like an outsider.

Finally, in November 2015, I couldn't ignore my gut's pull to Lebanon any more. My then partner Maria and I spent three weeks travelling around a country smaller than Sydney. We spent days and nights in Beirut, where brand new four-wheel drive Porsches battled it out in tiny alleyways with thirty-year-old Mercedes. Horns rang out incessantly, as if the whole city drove with one palm on the horn, the other out the window holding a cigarette. As pedestrians we had to be careful not to catch a foot on protruding cement or steel from buildings that were being demolished, their scarred bullet holes and mortar shell histories crumbling to the ground to make way for extravagant residences that only oil-rich Saudis could afford.

In Beirut we stayed in Hamra, the almost-hipster part of the city, in a large apartment we rented from a perpetually stoned young Lebanese Parisian. The apartment was big and airy, and we heard the call to prayer every morning and throughout the day, using it as a way to assess the time. Sometimes when we showered in the strangely briny water that left salt on our skin and in our hair, we would get small electric shocks from the taps, screaming out as the jolt pulsed through us.

Wandering streets that were sometimes reminiscent of Europe, sometimes of a war zone, we gave as much money as we could to thin, crying Syrian and Palestinian children to assuage our guilt. And there were so many, too many. There are over one and a half million Syrians and Palestinians trying to eke out a living in Lebanon, a country with a population of six million.

The tension between the Lebanese and the refugees is palpable and ever-present. Walking past a massive refugee camp next to ancient ruins, it's hard not to be struck by the collision of old and new civilisations, raising the question: how far have we actually come?

At night, Beirut really comes alive, its streets swarming with young men in tight jeans and even tighter T-shirts, women dressed to the nines with heavy eyeliner, straightened hair and heels dangerously precarious on the uneven pavement. Many sit and smoke the *argileh* in cafés and bars where loud music plays. There are familiar chains too, opening stores in a nation intent on proving it is once again the Paris of the Middle East.

As much as I loved that city, it was painfully obvious to me that I was something alien walking the streets. People would stop and stare, a butch dyke an unseen sight in that city, that country. There was never anything malicious expressed; in fact, people looked mostly shocked, often bursting into gleeful laughter. The Lebanese are not known for their social diplomacy and so, not knowing I could understand the language (if not speak it), they would talk loudly to each other about how I was actually a woman. One old man whose antique store we wandered into looked me up and down.

'You're a woman?' he asked.

'Yes, I sure am.'

'But that's impossible!' he replied, laughing heartily and clapping me on the back, a look of wonder on his face.

I never felt unsafe there, but there is no doubt that being an unending source of good-natured mirth instantly drove a wedge between the Lebanese and me. It was hard to truly connect with people and it made it uncomfortable, and incredibly exhausting at times, to just walk down the street. On some days, we'd sit on our balcony drinking tea, writing and listening to the call to prayer as it punctuated the day, unable to face the barrage of stunned faces on the street.

•

After our time in Beirut, where we stood on ruins that were nine thousand years old and ate food made from recipes as old as that too, where we talked to shopkeepers about politics and religion, conversed with taxi drivers about civil war and survival, refugees and perceptions of the West, we decided to head south to the Hezbollah museum. This had always been part of our travel plan, to see this war memorial built almost like some bizarre, propagandist theme park.

We had just driven out of the city when a bomb blast hit and killed forty-three people. People who love and laugh and fuck and dance and work and play and live just like us. But there was no Facebook button to click to let the world know we were safe, or that our new friends were safe, because somehow those lives mattered less. Lebanon mattered less. It made our trip to the Hezbollah museum even more intense, throwing into relief the precariousness of peace.

Once there, we walked through the tunnels and underground bunkers of the resistance; we saw Israeli tanks, their gun barrels tied in knots; we watched horrific multimedia presentations of the resistance in action and the subsequent forced withdrawal of Israel after an eighteen-year-long occupation. The gift shop was full of Hezbollah merchandise and I couldn't help but buy a T-shirt.

Later we travelled further south to Tebnine, my father's village. A dry, almost arid landscape strewn with rocks, just wet enough to water the fig and olive trees that grew in abundance along the roadside and next to villagers' houses. Ancient cobblestone lanes that could barely fit a single car wound up through the village, which itself straddled a small hill. Crusaders stayed in this town for years; there are still the remnants of a castle. Something sacred broke open in me as I walked Tebnine's steep paths, up towards the highest point. I stood in a turret of that old crumbling castle and looked down on what was once the Palestinian border. I thought of my great-grandfather who fled across that line and the millions of others since. It's hard to fathom the extent of loss and trauma that eventuates from such a brutal occupation, but even so, something moved in me as I stared wide-eyed at my father's homeland, looking down on the country of some of my ancestors.

After our time in the south, Maria and I decided to do an 80-kilometre trek across the north of Lebanon, against the advice of many Lebanese, to whom trekking is a very foreign and white idea. It was incredible. Over five days we climbed challenging mountains. From the peaks we could glimpse the sea, peer down into tiny villages where acorn trees, large and leafy, shaded ancient churches only big enough to fit a handful of people, still tended lovingly by local believers.

We entered cedar forests that have been standing for thousands of years and I sat on the branch of a cedar that was estimated to be two thousand years old. I asked it to hold me for a moment, then I held it, wrapped my arms around it, felt it hum, exchanged light with it.

We walked into the holy Qadisha Valley, where hermits reside in twelfth-century monasteries built into the mountainside. We climbed a precarious peak to visit one of the oldest living hermits, and the only one to accept visitors. A weathered man with crinkly eyes and an easy smile, he was deep in conversation with a group of nuns from the order of Mother Teresa when we arrived. Once he finished speaking to them, he walked over to us and took an instant liking to Maria.

'This might be paradise, but with you it would be heaven,' he said. Somewhat taken aback, we weren't sure how to deal with a sleazy hermit, so we descended the perilous cliff face as swiftly as we dared.

We ate apples from abandoned orchards, figs by Roman roadsides, rested our aching legs next to dancing, gurgling streams, eating cold *manoosh* for lunch. We met iPhone-holding shepherds, and shotgun-toting hunters who were fierce at first glance, with their camouflage gear and big beards, but who would break into shy smiles and say in thick accents, 'Welcome to Lebanon.' We stayed with local villagers who fed us until we were sure we might actually explode, sleeping in dusty rooms that were once filled with other travellers, during a time before civil war.

Throughout our entire journey, even with the confusion and shock at my masculine appearance, I was struck by the generosity and openness of the Lebanese. I felt a strong connection to the land, sky, sea and city, but still it was painfully evident that even here I was an outsider. I didn't belong.

After our trek, we headed back to Beirut, where we planned to meet up with a few queers I'd managed to connect with. Finding queers in Lebanon – in fact, finding queer Arabs at all – can be tricky. Some years ago, a friend of mine had introduced me to a secret online group run by queer Arab women, for queer Arab women. Through this group, I managed to make contact with quite a few Lebanese queers, including an amazing couple, Zabian and Toufie. They had met in America when they were both living there and had decided to move back to Lebanon together. Additionally, Zabian had an African-American child whom she'd adopted before the two had started dating. These brave women were raising an adopted black child in a country racist towards anyone darker than themselves, a country where nearly every middle-to-upper-class household has an Indian or Filipino housemaid, in a nation where it is illegal to be gay. They were – still are – trailblazers. Women just living as they feel they should be, carving a path for those in the future. They do it out of love for each other, the love for their child and their love of Lebanon.

They spoke of the upcoming parent–teacher night, the way their respective families dealt with their 'lifestyle' (two friends sharing an apartment, with separate rooms), how their house-keeper was discreet. They had no intention of endangering their family by being out. I thought back to my own coming out, how traumatic it was, how unnecessary at the time, and the amount of pressure heaped on me by white gays to be out and proud, without understanding any of the context of my culture.

On our last day they invited us to their sunny Hamra apartment for breakfast. We were joined by two of their queer female friends – Carol, a Palestinian filmmaker, and Aila, a psychotherapist. We ate *manoosh* with *zartar*, haloumi and olives, we drank cup after cup of strong Lebanese coffee and we talked about what it is to be queer and Lebanese. We discussed how simply living our lives in this way, whether out or not, was a form of resistance against perceived ideas of who we are and should be within our own cultures, but mostly against the continued colonisation and stereotypes perpetuated by the West.

Sitting in that apartment, talking Queerness, existence and art, it hit me. It hit me so hard I experienced a beautiful tearing in my chest, an opening I didn't even know existed. I listened to these fierce, intelligent, intellectual women, each doing their own bit of existing, fighting, resisting from the edges and I felt it. I felt a deep sense of belonging I had never experienced before.

This was my tribe.

I thought about how I am surrounded by bold Queer Arabic women, in Sydney, online and around Australia and the world, who have also expressed their feelings of not belonging. I thought about how lucky I was to have those connections, to be sisters with a global group who make the borderlands a place of belonging. It dawned on me that we occupy those fringes together. That we utilise things like art and activism to create a place of belonging within the margins and can revel in what it means to be outsiders who belong.

Candy Royalle

Candy Royalle was an award-winning writer, performance artist, poet, storyteller, activist, educator and vulnerability advocate. Candy's album *Birthing the Sky, Birthing the Sea*, a collaboration with the band The Freed Radicals, explored a fusion of rock and roll, funk, experimental soundscapes, hip hop, poetry with song.

She published two solo collections, *Love Spectacular* and *Heartbeats*, and toured extensively in Australia, the UK, Canada and the USA, with performances at Sydney Writers Festival, The Stella Awards, Austin International Poetry Festival, The Latitudes Festival in Toronto, and Woodford Folk Festival, to name a few. Her poetry and opinion pieces were published by Fairfax, SBS, *Overland*, *Mascara Literary Review*, *Peril*, *Australian Love Poems*, RN's Poetica, Austin Poet's International's *Di-vêrsé-city* anthology, *Butch Is Not a Dirty Word* magazine and many more.

Sadly, Candy passed away in June 2018 from ovarian cancer. She is remembered by her family and the LGBTQIA+ community for her strength, conviction and passion, and she will be deeply missed. A new collection of Candy's poems, *A Tiny Trillion Awakenings*, will be published by UWAP in November 2018.

BODILY INTERVENTIONS

Jax Jacki Brown

'm topless as I write this. It's officially the first day of summer and my nipple piercings glint in the sunlight streaming through the bay windows of our lounge room. I'm topless not because I'm hot, or because I'm trying to look 'extra queer' with my top off, but because I'm attempting to proclaim my queerness, DIY style.

I am re-dyeing my hair before going out to a queer event tonight. My 'dyke spike' is an essential part of my identity and a visible statement of my belonging to the LGBTIQA+ community and it must be in top form as I enter that dimmed room full of cool queers. I have a curfew, though; I must be home in time to acquire some fresh bruises, given to me – consensually, of course – by my girlfriend.

I examine my current collection. They are splotched across my belly, purple and yellow. Tonight, Anne will say, 'Are you ready?' as she draws up the needles, waiting for my consent before she plunges them in, the biggest of the three resisting, pulling on my skin before it finds its way through. I will catch my breath and try not to move.

I want to say that I'm unfazed, that I'm cool and calm and collected. That I lie with my hands behind my head, poised and sure of myself even in these quick moments of pain. I've got nipple and clit piercings, for fuck's sake. Why does my heart race when she does this to me? Perhaps it's because of the ramifications and enormity of what we are doing, and what this act could mean for our future.

We are flooding my body with IVF hormones.

When we looked into how we wanted to try and make a small human, Anne suggested partner IVF, where the egg from one person is placed in the womb of the other. She really wants to carry, and I have no desire to at all. Anne is also really into carrying a baby that is part of me. We don't know any cisgender men we're close enough with to ask them to be our donor, so DIY was not an option, and reciprocal IVF seemed like a way for us to both physically be involved in the process of making a baby.

We are dreaming of a queer future, a queer family, a cat, a house in the suburbs.

Is having a baby and living in the suburbs a radical act? Am I subverting this hetero norm by being queer? By being disabled? By doing sexuality, gender and parenting differently? By being a valued partner and hopefully kickarse parent in a society that tells people with disabilities that we cannot be either of these two things?

•

Anne and I met through an online dating app, although she had seen me do poetry at a queer performance night a few months earlier (see, poetry does get you the babes). I cruised her online and said, 'Hey, you're a bit cute.' Yeah, I know, original opener. We chatted for about a week before we met up.

She started leaving a stash of spare clothes at my house after eleven days of sleeping over, hiding the stash in one of the tall cupboards so I wouldn't find out and think it was a bit too much, too soon. A few weeks later, I generously cleared out a nook in my cupboard for her things, and she just ducked into the other room, returning with her sneaky armful of clothes.

We bought a tiny cactus together after a month or two, which we called 'the cactus of tiny commitment'. We worked out early on that we are both massive dorks! I know . . . it's sickeningly sweet.

Sure, there are some tensions, like she's a cat person and I'm very much on the dog side of the queer fence. But despite our differences, it's always just worked. Anne gives me a soft, safe space to land, a home filled with rainbow things and a future filled with love, friends and exciting possibilities.

I do remember asking if she was keen on kids somewhere in the sleep-deprived sex haze of those first few months, but it would be a few years before this part of our journey would become a priority.

Growing up I never thought I would have a future. As a young person with a disability I just didn't see people like me anywhere. If people with disabilities were shown on TV it was as objects of pity or tragedy, or conversely as inspirational, but never as complex, full human beings, living interesting and fulfilling lives. I had no role models to look up to and think, 'I could be doing what she's doing when I'm older.' I never saw wheelchair users having relationships, meaningful work, having kids . . . going to wild parties.

Queerness or any form of sexuality was not something that was considered an option for me. Disability is widely seen to be undesirable – an undesirable experience to endure and an undesirable trait in another person. It would, my parents told me, 'take a special kind of man to love you'. It didn't occur to them that someone could love me not in spite of my disability but because of it; that I could love and be proud of my body; or that maybe I wouldn't be into men.

Coming out as queer and claiming my disabled identity, learning to call this body home – just as it is, with pride instead of shame – is a radical act of reclamation and resistance in a society that tells people with disabilities that we should feel ashamed of who we are.

I remember the day I found my very first book on disability rights. I had just turned nineteen and was wheeling down the aisle of my small regional library, past the LGBTIQA+ books – which were categorised under 'deviance' – and on to the small disability section. I picked up a book called *Exploring Disability: A Sociological Introduction*. It was in its pages that I first encountered the 'social model' of disability – the idea that much of the disadvantage people with disability experience is due not to our bodies and minds being different, but because society is inaccessible. In this radical reframing, being disabled becomes a sociopolitical issue of identity and a fight for equal rights, similar to LGBTIQA+ experience. Looking back, it wasn't the most intersectional book, written by three wheelchair users who were white, straight, middle-aged men, but it really did transform my thinking – and the course of my life.

Around this time, I also gatecrashed my local university's women's collective. I wasn't at uni yet but I knew I needed to be around people who were thinking politically about identities. Also, if the rumours were true, the women's room was where all the lesbians were. The women's collective organised a conference and, at my insistence, flew up a seasoned disability activist who presented a keynote. She spoke about disability not as a personal issue but as an issue of human rights and justice. I sat in the aisle of the lecture theatre with goosebumps slowly covering my limbs; there were other people out there who were thinking in this bold, radical way!

I met and made friends with the disability representative on the student council, who lived by herself just a few streets away from me. She was in her early thirties but had only recently discovered the social model and it was beginning to change her thinking about herself and the world too. We would spend hours in her tiny flat each week, drinking cups of tea and discussing the ideas within the few books we could find, exploring blogs and websites on the disability rights movement in the US and the UK, wondering if it was going to come here, and how we could be part of it.

I distinctly remember going into the CBD of my small country town, wheeling up to this great gift shop that everyone raved about, looking up the flight of stairs to its entrance and thinking, 'I am not wrong. These stairs are the problem. This shop shouldn't be built this way.' This moment was revolutionary for me. I felt I was seeing the world anew: I felt angry at the lack of access instead of depressed about my body, but I also felt intrinsically connected to other disabled people. They were my people, and together we could advocate for change.

The medical profession does not view disability as a social issue but as a medical problem to be cured, minimised or eradicated. I spent my entire childhood immersed in this medicalised view of my body. Treatment to try and minimise my disability was the focus of my parents, doctors and therapists. My treatment started when I was diagnosed at two years old and consisted of very painful daily stretching of all my muscles, which are naturally very tight, by my mother and specialised therapists. I endured hours and hours of pain every day. I learned to cope by imagining myself above myself, looking down; from up there I was safe and I could endure whatever they decided to do to me; whatever they declared was in my 'best interests'. My body didn't belong to me, at all. It was the property of the medical profession. A project in normalisation.

I was placed into a special school at the age of three, where the sole focus was trying to unbend my naturally bent body. I remember once, and only once, I managed to 'run' past the therapy room to my classroom and escape my morning pre-class therapy session. I was tracked down by Carla, my therapist, and subjected to extra 'treatment' for all of recess.

My schoolwork was done while strapped in a painful standing frame for hours at a time. No one seemed to care about my mind or anything I was interested in or good at – just my body and trying to straighten me out.

One of my classmates was locked up behind a gate up the end of the outside area near our classroom, and left to wet his pants and cry and yell until he quieted down. He was sent there because he had autism and was sometimes loud, and would throw things. This cage was called 'time-out' and if you weren't well behaved you were sent there. I told Mum one day that this was where the naughty kids went. Mum phoned his mum, and then he wasn't at school anymore. The school had never told his family that this was his 'behavior management'. They didn't tell the parents all the things they did to us, all the 'techniques' they had for keeping us compliant. Me, I was a good girl. They could hurt my body as much as they liked and I didn't even cry.

So much damage is done to children with disabilities in the name of our presumed 'best interests', in order to bring us closer to this idea of normality. No one dares call what is done to our bodies, over and over, without our consent, child abuse. To my knowledge – and I have researched – there have been no studies looking into the long-term mental health impacts of undergoing years of treatments for impairments which will be lifelong and relatively unchanging. These pointless treatments dominated my childhood and left me with a very negative view of my body, as wrong and as fundamentally flawed and broken. How do you learn to love and value yourself when you have only been taught shame?

It has taken me years to reclaim my body from this medical discourse, to develop a different perspective on who I am and recognise my value to society. So coming from these experiences it was really difficult for me to give my body over again to the medical profession, especially for something as important and life-altering as having a child.

At the information night at the fertility clinic, the nurse tells us about the genetic tests they run on all donor sperm, and how, for an extra fee, they can run genetic tests on us and any of our future embryos to screen for Down syndrome, cystic fibrosis, haemophilia A, Tay–Sachs disease and two types of intersex variations, Turner and Klinefelter syndromes. As a queer person with disabilities, learning that parts of the communities to which I belong and which I value are actively being screened out is shocking and saddening, but we maintain a brave face throughout the session. We also find out that all donor sperm in Victoria is pre-tested for cystic fibrosis, fragile X syndrome, spinal muscular atrophy and thrombophilia, and that we can't opt out of this screening; that only sperm free of these conditions is made available. I tell the nurse we don't want to be tested and that we won't be screening any embryos. I say, 'Disability is part of human variation', and she leans across the table and grabs Anne's hand, looks her in the eye and says, 'But it's your choice. Is that want you want?'

We go to a prospective queer parents group and an IVF specialist comes and gives a presentation about their services. Someone asks how they can prevent disability. I am sitting right beside her. I am the visceral fear in the room for these queers; I am the terrible thing that could happen to their future children. I feel invisible and hypervisible at the same time.

We – our radical, political queer community – are enacting eugenics and calling it choice and we are paying big bucks for it. We are political about so many facets of our lives; critical about how society decides what is deemed 'normal' or acceptable. Yet as a community we often do not apply the same critical lens to disability. When I hear from fellow queers that they would do anything to avoid having a child like me, I feel the sting of otherness twofold. Eugenics is the pointy end of ableism but it comes in many more subtle forms: in queer events being held at inaccessible venues; in the common use of ableist slurs; by people assuming Anne must be my carer, or some kind of saint for choosing to be with me.

We go home from the information night feeling overwhelmed and sad at how much money our first round is going to cost – $15 000 – as we are not eligible for the Medicare rebate for our first round. If we were heterosexual we could say we had been trying to 'conceive naturally' without success for 18 months, and Medicare would deem us medically infertile. Instead, we are deemed 'socially infertile'. Surely, a lack of testicles/not having the bits to make a baby together is a pretty big medical issue.

Skip forward a couple of months. I am lying in recovery, alone, barely able to open my eyes; our specialist stands beside the bed and says, 'How are you feeling? A bit sore? We didn't get the result we'd hoped for. We only got three eggs, a lot less than we expected for your age, but hopefully they're all mature and all fertilise.'

I manage to squeeze out an 'okay'. She leaves and I start to cry. I'm not a big crier. Those years of painful therapy mean I find it hard to allow myself to cry. But I'm really crying now. A nurse comes over and says, 'Are you okay?' and I say, 'No, we didn't get many eggs' and she tells me, 'It's okay, you can try again next time.'

'Next time?' I want to shout. 'We just spent fifteen thousand dollars!' I say I want to see my partner, but she tells me to pull myself together; that she won't wheel me out until I've stopped crying.

'Your partner doesn't need to see you like this.'

All of the eggs fertilise, but only one makes it to day three and is transferred into Anne. The embryo transfer costs another $2500. We wait the two weeks to find out if we're pregnant; it happens to be the two weeks right before Christmas. We were so optimistic going into this – we thought we were going to be pregnant by Christmas, or at least have a stockpile of eggs for the new year. The embryo doesn't take and we are devastated.

We book an appointment to see our specialist and I ask why she thinks we got so few eggs. She says she doesn't know; maybe my body wasn't responding to the hormones. She also admits that our embryo didn't look that healthy and that it may have even stopped growing before the transfer. Why then, I ask, did she transfer it? 'We find we have to transfer something into a woman each cycle, otherwise she might not come back,' she replies.

We feel too broken to be angry. I go and see a queer counsellor, thinking, *Well, at least she'll get the queer stuff, even if I have to play disability 101 with her*. She tells me her rooms are accessible, but when I arrive they are not, so she has to carry my wheelchair down some steps. I briefly tell her about round one and she asks, 'How do you feel when your body fails you?' I begin to cry because this question is so loaded with her assumptions: assumptions about my body failing me because I'm disabled and about IVF being a failure of the body. I just want to leave but I can't get out without her 'help'. She tells me I won't really be in touch with my emotions until I can feel where failure sits in my body. I am too emotionally exhausted to try and outline why her 'approach' doesn't work for me.

I try and find as many first-person accounts of IVF as I can, but there are not many out there. It's such an intensely personal thing to go through, so all-consuming, that many people find it hard to write or talk about publicly. Either you get the baby in the end and don't want to revisit such a difficult time, or you don't have a child and it's just too painful to talk about.

Infertility is widely perceived as a personal problem, a failure of the body, a private struggle, an individual issue we should hide and feel ashamed about. The more I research, the more I see that this cultural narrative is very similar to the way we think of disability. Slowly, this realisation allows me to view what we are going through in a politicised way, moving through my feelings of hopelessness to productive activist anger.

IVF shouldn't be so expensive and it should be subsidised for those who need it. Fertility clinics should be mandated to publish and make freely available their statistics, informing people of their actual chances of success. It is unacceptable that it has become legislated practice to screen out disabilities and intersex variations without public discussion and debate.

I start talking about what I'm going through publicly and I get connected with some people who have been through it too and are critical of the industry and how it treats us and our bodies. I am not alone.

Maybe my low egg yield is my body refusing to play ball with the medical profession: a big 'Fuck you, I won't do what you tell me!'

When I finally call the clinic to discuss new treatment for a second round, I am placed on hold and a pre-recorded message informs me: 'We are here to give you quality service and assist you in your dream of having a baby.'

Not everyone gets a baby, but the whole industry is built on selling this hope – a happy, healthy, 'normal' baby will be yours if you just hand over enough money.

I book in an appointment and go and see one of the clinic's nurses to ask what my options are. 'Just try and stay positive,' she says as she escorts me out. I remember the quote by disability activist Stella Young: 'No amount of smiling at a flight of stairs has ever made it turn into a ramp.' I need a pithy comeback to this positive attitude bullshit.

We do a second round and get four eggs this time; three fertilise and they all make it to day three, so they can be frozen and then individually transferred into Anne. By the time we transfer the last embryo we are both exhausted, depressed and have truly given up hope. We had talked about flushing the embryo or leaving it frozen indefinitely, but neither of us can deal with those options so we put it in.

Our last little embryo takes! Anne does a test at home and sees a faint positive, so she rushes into town to meet me, little stick in her handbag. We both stare at the positive line and convince ourselves that the process has sent us over the edge and we are not really pregnant but have some shared delirium. Anne keeps peeing on pregnancy test sticks until we get a positive blood test, and even after.

By the time this book is published there will be a tiny human in our lives, but we are still angry. There needs to be more people talking about the industry and the pain it causes, to critically engage with its problems and start to address the inequities. Queerness and queer family-making is about more than love and sexuality; it's about access, inclusion and equality.

Jax Jacki Brown

Jax Jacki Brown is a disability and LGBTQI activist, writer, public speaker and disability sexuality educator. Jax holds a BA in Cultural Studies and Communication where she examined the intersections between disability and LGBTQI identities and their respective rights movements.

Jax is a co-producer of Quippings: Disability Unleashed a disability performance troupe in Melbourne. She has written for *Junkee*, *Daily Life*, *The Feminist*

Observer, Writers Victoria, ABC's *Ramp Up* and in print for *Hot Chicks with Big Brains, Archer Magazine: The Australian Journal for Sexual Diversity, Queer Disability Anthology* and *Doing It: Women Tell the Truth About Great Sex.* She can be found on **@jaxjackibrown**.

UNDER THE WIRE

Ginger Valentine

'm not the most sexual person you'll ever meet. In fact, I'm about as erotically charged as an episode of *Frasier*. I find it hard to listen to Prince, and I still squirm at sex scenes in movies like you did when you were nine. I understand now that sex is not my thing, but it took an awfully long time for me to figure that out. It wasn't until I was in my thirties that I started to understand what asexuality meant, and it was a few years more before I could use the word to describe myself.

In my early twenties, I told my parents that I wouldn't be eating meat any more (bear with me here – I'm not saying we should add a 'V' for vegetarian to LGBTQIA+). For most of my adult life, I'd only been eating meat occasionally, and even then only in specific cases. I decided to stop completely when I realised I wasn't enjoying it, and was actively choking down the odd bit of fish to save Mum from having to cook yet another separate meal for me. Both my parents, separately from one another, took this announcement without surprise. 'Oh, I've been waiting for you to say that,' Mum said. 'You've never liked eating meat – even as a baby, you'd try to throw it back up if we made you swallow it.' Once I'd gotten old enough to see what everyone else was doing, though, I fell in line. I'd barbecue sausages until they were black tubes of carbon, and drown them in sauce. I knew my tastes weren't like those of my omnivorous family, but I tried so hard to fit in that I fooled myself.

Sex was the same. For me, sex is like *The Wire* – I'm glad you like it, if that's your thing, but it's never done it for me. And just like that premium HBO drama, I thought I wanted it for years. It seemed like everyone talked about *The Wire* all the time, and . . . well, I got caught up in the hype. I bought all five seasons at once, sight unseen. It sat on my shelf for a while, and every now and again I'd see it and tell myself, 'I really should get stuck into that.' When I finally did, I gave it a red-hot go – I got about a third of the way into season two before I realised I wasn't all that interested in watching the rest. I could see why others might get sucked in by the labyrinthine plot, or be pulled into the morally ambiguous world of policing the drug trade in Baltimore, but it just left me . . . cold.

If only I'd come to the same conclusion about sex as quickly as that. But, unfortunately, I wasn't so self-aware as a teenager (self-conscious, yes, but less adept with self-knowledge). Caught up in the stormy seas of hormones, peer pressure and hetero-normativity, I never stopped to wonder if sex was something that I actually wanted. It simply never crossed my mind; boys were supposed to want it, and girls were supposed to give it up lest they be dumped for being frigid. That was just how it was.

High school gossip revolved around who had had sex with whom, and there was a distinctly gendered value to that. Boys who'd done 'it' were mature, wise men of the world, while the girls were, of course, 'sluts', a word always whispered in scandalised tones dripping with moralistic horror. The fact that these judgements were mostly based on third-hand rumours or outright lies didn't change the fact that it was a burden to a teenage boy to still be a virgin at the ripe old age of sixteen, while girls were written off as ruined things for daring to want sex in their own right. Even then, my underdeveloped adolescent mind wondered at the startling misogyny of that attitude, but I didn't question it any more than I interrogated whether I actually liked the many Metallica albums I bought (maybe a little, but not really, for the record). I was 100 per cent on board the sex train. I thought it was the solution to all my problems; I'd be more confident, more mature, generally better liked, if only I'd had sex.

There was a disconnect between what I thought I should want and what I actually wanted. For all the talk – and despite the standard-issue mind-bending, world-ending teenage crushes – I never pursued sex, nor did I ever get close to having a romantic relationship.

There was one drunken teenage night where a girl brought me back to her house after we split a bottle of scotch (by which I mean I'd had maybe two shots). I remember her leading me upstairs to her bedroom, and we stood in the doorway talking softly for a few moments, her body inches from mine, before I abruptly said, 'Goodnight' too loudly and wandered downstairs to sleep soundly on her couch.

At the time, I put that down to having the physical and emotional grace of a baby giraffe, not to mention the same ability to read social cues. But while all those were probably factors, I saw my friends, most of whom were as clumsy and awkward as I was, partnering up over and over, while I never really tried. Despite my constant whingeing about it on early social media, it wasn't until I was at university that I finally kissed someone for the first time. When it finally happened, it was . . . fine? But it wasn't the life-changing event I'd been promised, and it would be years still before I bothered to kiss anyone else, let alone date.

By this point, I'm in my late twenties and still a virgin. That should've been a hint that I maybe wasn't that interested in 'it'. Like that *Learn Japanese the Easy Way* instructional DVD that is gathering dust in everyone's house, it didn't happen because I didn't do anything about it. Of course, that didn't stop me from building my self-worth around the fact that I hadn't had sex; by then, I was certain that it was a character flaw, a sign that something was wrong with me rather than a choice I had unconsciously made for myself.

Movies like *The 40-Year-Old Virgin* made it clear that I was somehow wrong; that I'd missed an important part of growing up, and that getting laid was the only thing that could save me. I internalised all that without question, and the self-loathing only isolated me further. It became my trademark – looking back, it feels like I was forever telling people how horrible and unloveable I was, and I'd like to pay special commendation to the friends who knew me then and still like me now, even after living through that phase.

In spite of all those hang-ups, I eventually stumbled into my first real relationship aged twenty-seven, and sex was an inescapable part of that. Finally, I was sure this burden would be lifted, and I'd transform, caterpillar-style, into a well-rounded and mature member of society. I'd be normal.

From our very first night together something was wrong. I struggled to engage. Physically, everything worked as it should, but I couldn't connect. *Is this what sex is supposed to feel like?* I thought. *Is this what everyone's obsessed with?* I mean, sex is fine, but have you ever had a fresh undercut with hair hanging loose over the top? I could believe everyone being fixated on that feeling, but I just could not muster the energy to care. This thing that I had yearned for, that I thought would make me a complete human at last, just left me . . . cold. Maybe there was something wrong with me. Maybe I wasn't doing it right. I didn't understand what was happening, so I persisted, trying to give my partner what they needed, hoping that it'd all make sense eventually.

My partner and I carried on that way for a few years, but we both knew something was amiss. In our years together, we almost never fought, but the toughest nights were when we'd argue about our sex life, or the lack thereof. My partner was hurt, thinking that it was something about them that I found undesirable. I couldn't explain to them that that wasn't it; that the problem was, I thought, with me. I didn't have the words, or the self-knowledge, to make sense of it, so how could I expect them to understand?

Of all places, I was on an airbed in Edinburgh, jet-lagged and scrolling through Twitter, when a friend helped me find the words I'd been looking for. She talked about getting drunk enough to let boys have sex with her, just to keep them happy, and how tired she was of living like that. She sent me links to some things she'd been reading, and I recognised myself instantly: not just the lack of interest in sex, but the taser-like jolt of awkwardness that goes through my body when sex is discussed or, God help me, initiated. I'd heard of asexuality before, but I didn't fully understand it – all I knew was that it had something to do with Morrissey, and that wasn't really a selling point for me. I'd never thought it might apply to me, or help me understand myself. But in that moment, I understood that I wasn't broken, or damaged by trauma, or missing an essential part of what it means to be human. All of a sudden, I wasn't alone.

I'd like to say that everything was fixed in that moment, but I'd be lying. As G.I. Joe once said, knowing is half the battle. The second half of that battle lasted a long time, if it's even finished at all. It would be a few more years and a few more fights before my partner and I worked out what my sexuality meant for our relationship. I encouraged them to consider polyamory early on, since it seemed ridiculous to me that their lust should be held in or denied entirely just because I wasn't interested in sex. They were reluctant at first, and with good cause – polyamory isn't a quick-fix solution, and it has its own risks and challenges. They resisted, and I didn't push, but the fights kept happening. Every few months, after the drought had gone on too long for them to bear, we'd find ourselves shouting at one another in stage whispers as we tried to have a frank conversation about our respective sexual needs without waking the baby sleeping just steps away.

Finally, as we wondered out loud if we needed to break up, I accused my partner of not taking my sexuality seriously. I asked if it would be easier if I was gay; if they'd still expect the same of me then. And even though neither of us knew how to answer that question out loud, we knew then in the quiet that we'd had a breakthrough. Within a few weeks, we'd discussed polyamory again. We set out the preliminary rules by which we'd operate (they would go on dates and have sex; I would make podcasts), and quickly found out that them dating outside of our relationship actually made us stronger. It took the pressure off sex, and meant the midnight fights stopped completely.

That epiphany wasn't the end for me as an individual, either. If anything, it sparked a line of thought that I'm still working through today. Even as I'm less and less interested in the physical act of sex, it's hard to separate that from the other cultural values we place on it – it's so tied up in tenderness, intimacy, validation, power, status, and a million other things. I find myself occasionally wanting sex while not wanting to have sex. Unpacking all that and how it applies to me as a person is a knotty process that I'll probably never be done with. And it's not just sex – how many other parts of myself, parts that I take as given, were socialised rather than arising naturally? Separating nature and nurture is an almost impossible task, but it's set me questioning my sexuality, my gender, and a host of other things I accepted as normal for too long.

That's why I've started going by Ginger now instead of my birth name – the identity assigned to me at birth never really fit, and I'm just now, in my mid-thirties, stopping to figure out who I am, without the burden of socialised expectations. I don't know if I'll ever be able to fully answer those questions; they'll probably just open up yet more questions.

But I do know one thing for sure: I'm selling a box set of *The Wire*, if anyone's interested.

Ginger Valentine

Ginger Valentine is a writer, a podcaster and a pop-culture commentator, pastimes that feel as natural to them as breathing. And, like breathing, they'll keep doing it even when no one's listening. You can buck the trend, and listen to their podcast, *Common Sense with Burt Franklap,* at **gingerBFG.com**. When they're not at a computer, you can usually find them chasing their toddler around the pubs and cafés of Melbourne's Inner North.

They tweet at **@gingerBFG**.

DEAR AUDRE

Candy Bowers

dedicate this piece to my greatest lover: the Black, lesbian poet, educator and author Audre Lorde (1934–1992).

That is how I learnt that if I didn't define myself for myself, I'd be crunched into other people's fantasies for me and eaten alive.

Audre Lorde

October 2016

Dear Audre,

Today I played Miriam Makeba's version of Solomon Linda's 'The Lion Sleeps Tonight' for my students. I have designed a class called Decolonising Theatre and I begin it with Mama Africa's music. In its original context, 'The Lion Sleeps Tonight' was a mourning song, a message stick letting the village know that their King had died. 'The King is dead tonight' is a better translation, so the French version is the most accurate: *'Le lion est mort ce soir.'*

For me, the appropriation of the song by sixties doo-wop vocal group The Tokens is an excellent case study in how the white man took African culture and reinterpreted it in order to put their minds at ease.

In the popular version we are comforted because the lion is asleep. In the popular version the lion is something to fear. But in the original, the lion was our leader and our chief; his death caused so much grief that the villagers wept.

Sometimes I feel like the grim reaper, killing my students' childhood joys, one beloved memory at a time. 'Don't get me started on Pocahontas' would quickly turn into a full-blown rant about how disturbing it was for Disney to turn a tragedy – the capture of a young Indigenous woman by an old white man – into a love story. It wasn't love: it was rape and it was slavery . . . And how confusing to have Vanessa Williams, an African-American woman, sing the theme song: 'Cos, like, any brown female will do, right? We're all inter-changeable.' My interventions have not always been welcome or well received, but Audre, you taught me to speak my truth no matter how unwelcome.

The learning process is something you can incite, literally incite, like a riot.

Audre Lorde

December 2001

Dear Audre,

Yesterday, I graduated as an actor after three years of blood, sweat and tears at the National Institute of Dramatic Arts (NIDA) and today, I failed on entry. I have no prospects and no agents want to represent me. I was told by a series of casting folks that I will not get work on the Australian stage or screen. We didn't talk about my talents or dreams; we spoke only of my appearance.

I challenged them and said, 'But I was born here.' I said, 'There are plenty of roles for women out there and ain't I a woman?' When I was in high school I read Sojourner Truth's speech comparing the life of African-American women to White American women during the suffragist era. Back then I thought about the speech all the time, but I was too young to understand how I was living the double standard. Needless to say, no one cared for my quote or the parallel (Australian agents weren't particularly conscious of racism back then). The commercial Australian industry was not interested in a caramel brown, mixed-race Blasian South African woman with a size 16 booty. I guess I didn't look the part . . . any of them.

It is not our differences that divide us. It is our inability to recognize, accept, and celebrate those differences.

Audre Lorde

You were a Black woman, a Black lesbian no less, running rap and poetry workshops at libraries, speaking at universities and publishing books in 1970s America, in the thick of the Civil Rights movement. How did you do it? How did you survive? I'm done. It's too hard. I know you had it tougher than me, but, still, continuing seems futile. I am twenty-two years old and I feel utterly invisible.

> *Pain is important: how we evade it, how we succumb to it, how we deal with it, how we transcend it.*
>
> Audre Lorde

Is this apartheid? It's 2001 and the colour barrier at the entrance into the Australian stage and screen industry is real. I can't fulfil my dreams or ply my craft because I don't fit the frame. Should I keep trying even though I know I'm so terribly undesirable? Can I call myself an actor if I never act again?

What am I supposed to do with all of the characters inside me?

Like Sally's brown best friend on *Home and Away*: 'This potato salad's awesome Pip. Maybe Sal and I can take some to the boys playing volleyball on the beach later?'

Or that short round African-American bag lady that I met on Michigan Avenue on the first day of winter in Chicago last year. Her cigarette stuck to her lip as she tried to speak to me and light it at the same time: 'Every time I sit on the North Side, all the South Side buses come. Every time I sit on the South Side, all the North Side buses come. Don't you sit at the bus stop I'm sitting on, because yo' bus ain't never gon' come!'

Or the forty-year-old blonde white South African guy who I guessed was a personal trainer, having a tiff with his mum outside the supermarket on King Street in Newtown: 'Raisins, Mummy. Raisins! This is not the right muesli. I specifically said no dried fruit. I've explained this several times: *shredding = zero sugar*! Fruit is sugar, Mummy! Fructose, Mummy. All you needed to get was *fruit-free* muesli. Sometimes I don't know how you cannot keep simple concepts in your thick skull. Now I have to go in there mahself, return this box and get the right one . . . *mahself*. See, Mummy, if I can't rely on you to get the right one, I'm have to do it mahself.'

What am I gonna do with him? I really need to get him out of me.

Or the solarium-orange, thick-eyelashed ladettes who surrounded me in the bathroom when I went to see *The Lion King* in the West End in London: 'Are you related to someone in the cast? Are you related? Where are you from? Canada? . . . Australia? No way! You must be from Canada. Really, Australia? But there's no Black people in Australia. I watch *Home and Away* and *Neighbours* . . . You must be from Canada.'

There is a constant drain of energy which might be better used in redefining ourselves and devising realistic scenarios for altering the present and constructing the future.

Audre Lorde

May 2004

Dear Audre,

Today I saw a life-size poster of me in the front of the Sydney Opera House. My queer feminist hip-hop comedy act will be at the Sydney fucking Opera House for two weeks, performing in our first original production, *Inna Thigh – The Sista She Story*. Someone in the graphics team decided that a light green wash would work over the image, so the whole thing is a little 'under the seaweed' but you can still tell it's us . . . I mean, you can still see that I'm Black. In the poster I'm wearing a shiny Everlast white tracksuit, white Adidas and a visor: classic Western Sydney hip-hop attire. I'm not sure how many Aussie-born women from the Afro-Asian diaspora have had a billboard in front of the Opera House. It feels like a breakthrough. I feel alive.

No one was going to write a part for me, so I wrote one for myself. Rasheda MC Eda the Sista-Leader is a Blasian rapper from Campbelltown. I'm using my own accent and the show is set between Western Sydney and the Sutherland Shire, where Rasheda's partner in rhyme Sheila MC Eila the Harmonic Healer resides. It's a somewhat heightened slice of my real life . . . I mean, my real life if I'd met my hip-hop soulmate on a train station, bonded over being sexually harassed by a toothless man and gone on to become the first female rap team to gain SUPERSTARDOM in Australia. It's basically a documentary.

Sista She got spotted at a friend's queer Christmas cabaret at the Side On Hotel in Annandale in 2002. Six minutes was all it took for the executive producer Virginia Hyam to book us for a scratch night (a sort of testing ground) at the Opera House. One year later, we are preparing for our main stage debut. Lucky I picked myself up, huh?

There's a whisper on the streets, can you hear it through the trees? It's the rhythm of the sweet Sista, Lady, Girl MCee.

Sista She

January 2014

Dear Audre,

Tonight was big. We premiered 'Hot Brown Honey' at Woodford Folk Festival, and I performed my most bold character to date: Happy Ma'x'wewe. Discovered in a spotlight amongst the crowd, draped in kente cloth and head wrap, Happy Ma'x'wewe addressed her audience:

Hello, my name is Happy Ma'x'wewe and I am newly arrived. I see many similarities between my new home Australia and my homeland, South Africa. Now I would like to sing a song highlighting the similarities regarding the interconnected history of light-skinned women, colonisation and rape. It is a classic number. I wrote it last week.

As Happy moves through the crowd, beaming and greeting guests, a bright folksy guitar begins. The music is somewhat reminiscent of Miriam Makeba's during her Harry Belafonte phase. Happy mounts the stage, smiling she begins to sing:

> *No, it didn't take long for the Milky man*
> *To bring his milk from his milky van,*
> *To spread his cream right across the land.*
> *Nooooooo, it didn't take long for the Milky man.*

The Coloniser not only desired our land, they also desired our bodies. They did not ask, they simply took what they wanted, when they wanted it.

Here comes the chorus!

> *Milky, Milky, oh Milky Milky Man*
> *Milky, Milky, spread his cream across the land.*
> *Everybody join in with me!*
> *Milky, Milky, oh Milky Milky Man,*
> *Milky, Milky, spread his cream across the land.*

It's quite extraordinary seeing three hundred people dismantle in front of you. Ripples of shock and horror mixed with wide eyes and a sprinkle of even wider smiles (often from people of colour).

And once he came it was plain to see
He came to plant not to sow his seed.
Back to his own he would go, and we
Would sing of the days when we were free.

Milky, Milky, oh the Milky Milky Man,
Milky, Milky, spread his cream across the land.
Now how this ends has a twist you know,
Cos the Milkman's daughters began to grow
And as they grew, their milk it flowed
And they fed their Daddy's babies from below.

The Coloniser preferred light-skinned women inside the house. We washed their floors, we cooked their food and we fed our brothers and sisters with the milk from our titties. Now who is hungry? I am looking for a baby . . .

This was the moment I was most freaked out about. This wasn't just audience participation; it was immersive theatre, in which everyone in the room became complicit. Our heritage and ethic identities became inescapable. It was thrilling!

As Black women we live our herstory (our past and our ancestry) daily. In this moment I asked a white man to do the same.

Happy Ma'x'wewe seeks out a man of Dutch or English heritage in the crowd and she asks him his name, but no matter what he says, she calls him Colin – it's the name of the first white man she met at the airport and it's easier for her to remember. She dresses Colin in a nappy, bonnet and bib and sits him on her knee. She reveals her teats (a neon pink bra with baby bottle tops sewn on), places one in Colin's mouth and instructs him to drink (which he did with fervour, I might add).

While he suckles she invites the audience to gently serenade him . . .

Milky, Milky, oh the Milky Milky Man . . .

Then she says:

Now, Mr Andrew Bolt, or any other ignoramus vomit button out there, next time you question a light-skinned black person about their racial identity, ripping open the extraordinary wound of assimilation and multi-generational rape, I hope you will remember this moment!

The audience was a mix of titillation, shock and horror. They sang along and squeaked with laughter. Oh Audre, I broke all the rules and transformed the game. I am the latest model of my ancestry and the embodiment of my foremothers' wildest dreams!

The sharing of joy . . . forms a bridge between the sharers which can be the basis for understanding . . . and lessens the threat of their difference.

Audre Lorde

July 2015

Dear Audre,

Today, I am in South Africa and I am filled with every possible emotion. My face makes sense here. I see people who look like me everywhere. Round soft features, Afro hair, smiles as wide as a river and so much booty. Much more booty than I have, in fact. I'm jealous of all the booty here.

I'm soaking it all in: the accents, the multitude of languages spoken everywhere, the condensed milk, the pickled fish at the petrol station, and the politics; the wonderful difficult politics. I can have political conversations about equality, justice and the future of South Africa with any given person on the street. The theatre here is heart-wrenchingly brilliant. I'm in awe and in love, in shock and in hurt, in joy and in rage, daily. I'm attending symposiums, classes, talks and breakfasts as part of the Vryfees, the Festival of the Free State in Bloemfontein (which I'm pronouncing terribly wrong, like a true Aussie).

I overhear the artistic director of the festival and his boyfriend arguing over whether I am South African or Australian. The boyfriend couldn't understand how I could feel so South African, having grown up in Australia. I hear the AD say, 'It's about what she feels, not what you think.' The complexity of the diasporic African experience is great.

How do I feel?

I feel everything at the same time.

I feel the hunger for understanding my parents' home. Frankly, being on the ground here is electric. I feel connected, yet still outside, like enjoying a family opening presents on Christmas morning through the window before being invited in . . . Inside, there are so many familiar smells and objects. My family home has identical artwork and crockery, but the house sits on very different land.

Meeting the students from the University of the Free State is instrumental; I'm completely overwhelmed by this rich and talented group of majority Black young people. I want to teach in South Africa. On the way home to my hotel, I say to my driver (a student himself), 'I wonder what it would have been like to study acting surrounded by Black people . . .' I trail off, imagining the sliding door. We stop at the entrance. 'Better,' he says.

Sometimes we are blessed with being able to choose the time, and the arena, and the manner of our revolution, but more usually we must do battle where we are standing.

Audre Lorde

Right Now

Dear Audre,

You are and always have been my ultimate lover and protector. Your poetry has been my saviour, my hope, my anchor, my shoulder, my life jacket, my comfort, my oxygen and my wine. Every time the tide of woe has consumed me I've reached out for you and every time your words carried me back.

You died of cancer, just shy of your sixtieth birthday. You said, 'Life is very short and what we have to do must be done now.' From one Black Unicorn to another, I'm fearless, whole and real because you were.

Queer. Radical. Black. Unicorn.

Candy Bowers

Candy Bowers is an award-winning writer, actor, social activist, comedian and producer. The co-artistic director of Black Honey Company, Candy has pioneered a fierce sub-genre of hip hop theatre that delves into the heart of radical feminist dreaming. Born of multi-racial South African parents and raised in the Western Suburbs of Sydney, Candy studied at the National Institute of Dramatic Art (NIDA). Since then she has gone on to perform across the country and the world, and has appeared on the small screen in *Newton's Law* (ABC/ Netflix), *Tonightly with Tom Ballard* (ABC) and *Get Krack!n* (ABC/Netflix).

Her awards and accolades include the British Council of the Arts Realise Your Dream Award, Australia Council of the Arts Cultural Leadership Fellowship, Philip Parsons Young Playwright Award Short List, Melbourne Fringe Best Performance and Director's Choice Award, Adelaide Fringe Youth Education Award and The Geoffrey Milne Memorial Award for her ongoing work championing diversity and inclusivity in the arts.

She tweets at **@TheCandyBowers**.

BUILDING A HOUSEHOLD

Simon Copland

This is a story about building my household. In many ways my household is a normal one. We do a weekly shop, we negotiate – and sometimes we fight – about whose turn it is to do the dishes and who has to mop the floors this week. We've started a small vegetable garden (based entirely in pots in our front yard), and have bought a worm farm to deal with our food scraps.

But my household is also very different. Instead of living with my one 'soulmate', I live with my two partners: James and Martyn. While James and Martyn are good friends they are not romantically attached. So, in this household of ours, I decide which room I'll sleep in on a nightly basis. While we spend a lot of time doing things as a trio, I often need to find ways to spend time separately with each of them, making sure we make space to be both couples, and an amazing threesome.

Our household is different. This is the story of how we built it, and the values that underpin it. But it is also a story of what building this household did to our connection with the 'queer community', and in turn a cautionary tale about what happens when we start to abandon the values that are supposed to be the building blocks of our movement.

•

I first met James on Valentine's Day a week after I turned eighteen. It was my first week of university, and my brother and sister took me out to the O-week bar crawl. Boy, were they in for a shock. The night ended at Mooseheads, one of Canberra's biggest and most notorious nightclubs. Neither of us really remember exactly how, but somehow over the course of that crazy night, I met James.

The night is still a blur, but here are some highlights: James and I being asked by someone to stop making out, not because – as he very strongly pointed out – he had a problem with two guys making out, but because we were blocking the bar; James trying to impress me by sliding down the bannister of the stairs; and James hitting on a previous fling before he left. The pièce de résistance of our antics was James leaving, and then sending me a text saying, 'Why aren't you following me' when I didn't come home with him. Can you think of anything more romantic?

Despite our dodgy beginnings James and I quickly fell for each other. We instantly connected on an intellectual level. He stimulated and challenged me, and despite his somewhat brash exterior, he was, and remains, a sweetie underneath. He always had a smile on his face when he saw me.

James also opened up a whole new world for me. From the very beginning James was sceptical of long-term monogamous relationships, at one point telling me that he didn't really believe he could last in a relationship longer than three months. Coming out of high school, where all my friends were obsessed with getting boyfriends and girlfriends, I was genuinely shocked when he told me he had only ever had one boyfriend – a relationship that had lasted less than a couple of months too! James wanted our relationship to be 'open' – we could have sex with other people, as long as we were honest about it.

I had never really encountered this idea before, having spent my life socialised into the notion that monogamy was the only way to go. I was anxious about the idea of James sleeping with someone else; but at the same time, not quite sure yet where this relationship would lead, I figured I had little to lose. I was only eighteen, and while I wanted a relationship, I also didn't want to give up the sexual possibilities that came with my new-found adulthood. So I gave it a shot.

•

In our first year together I worked at a café near his apartment, and would drop in after I'd finished, sometimes past midnight, for quick cuddles before I drove home. By the next year we'd moved in together, and we haven't lived apart since (apart from times when, by arrangement, we've been in different cities). We did the normal relationship things – we travelled, we fought, we dealt with each other's emotional highs and lows, we joined the same political party (which on reflection is probably not a normal relationship thing for most people). We fell very much in love.

We also continued being open. After realising that this relationship was here to stay, I gave up my 'What's the worst that could happen?' mindset, and instead started to think about what being open actually meant. James and I spoke about how neither of us could realistically provide for all the sexual needs of the other, and that having one-off, occasional sexual encounters with other people did not diminish the love that we had for each other. We agreed that physical satisfaction does not have to be exclusive to just one person, and that having sex with other people could actually enhance our own sexual lives.

This situation was not entirely perfect. I would still get anxious and James would get frustrated at my anxiety. Sometimes we crossed boundaries that the other was not comfortable with, eventually leading us to create an agreement around our openness – we could only have sex once with someone we had a crush on; we could each veto the other person having sex with someone else if it crossed an emotional boundary; and we would always be honest about having sex with other people. This was also a part of our relationship that we kept to ourselves. We never told our family, and rarely told friends, fearful that it would lead to a backlash or, even worse, a judgement about how much we loved each other.

•

Things changed when we moved to Brisbane in 2012. James moved up at the start of the year to work on the Queensland state election, and I followed him soon after. In the state of Joh Bjelke-Petersen we started to hang out with a small group of radical queers, all of whom were in polyamorous relationships. These amazing women, who we became extremely close with, would sometimes be dating three or four people at once, and were extremely comfortable talking openly about their relationships with us. Soon we realised that our philosophy around having sex outside our relationship could extend to emotional relationships as well. Just as our relationship couldn't realistically provide for all of our sexual needs, it also mightn't emotionally. With us both having a few crushes here and there, we soon started to think about the possibility of being polyamorous.

Then we went to Edinburgh, and we met Martyn. It was our second night on a trip around Scotland, a cold, dark, windy and rainy evening. We'd travelled to the UK for the Men's Roller Derby World Cup, in which James was skating for the Australian team. Just before we set off I caught a cold, and with the jetlag now setting in, all I wanted to do was go back to our hostel and sleep. But James had organised for us to meet a friend of his – someone he had met on Tumblr through derby circles – and thinking that we wouldn't get another opportunity before we left, I ventured out.

We met Martyn at the Starbucks on the Royal Mile – a universal Edinburgh meeting point – and he took us to a small pub called the World's End. This place was historically at the edge of the city limits in old Edinburgh and Martyn likes to comment now that I looked like I was at my own World's End that night too. But I powered through. We had a drink or two, James and I had roast for dinner, and we chatted about derby, work and the cold Edinburgh evening. When we got back to our hotel I found that Martyn had added me as a friend on Facebook. Lying in bed we started chatting a little, a conversation that has not stopped yet.

We kept chatting online, flirting with each other like crazy. A few days after we first met, James, Martyn and I caught up for another drink in one of Edinburgh's best gay bars, then we encouraged him to come down to Birmingham for the weekend of the World Cup. Martyn's a schoolteacher so couldn't take any time off work, but agreed anyway, leaving Edinburgh on Friday afternoon to make the drive. That night, with James having gone to bed, Martyn and I hit the gay strip in Birmingham. In our first bar I encouraged him to give his number to a cute barman (again, so romantic!) and then after a few more drinks in our second bar we started making out. We went back to Martyn's hotel, hooking up, and then falling asleep. At about six I woke in an anxious panic, thinking James would be worried about where I was, and got Martyn to call me a taxi back to my hotel.

I felt a strong spark with Martyn from the moment I met him. We connected emotionally, and also quickly realised we had lots in common, bonding over music, books and politics. Martyn is smart, but in a different way to me, and he frequently challenges how I see the world. I got excited whenever I saw a message from him, a smile appearing on my face every time.

For the rest of my trip with James – to London, Jordan and Myanmar (a strange itinerary, I know, but it made sense to us), Martyn and I would chat as much as we could. I utilised the wi-fi in the IKEA in Amman to send him messages, and got frustrated when the internet at our hotel in a coastal Myanmar town was so slow I couldn't open Facebook. When we got back to Australia we kept chatting every day. We started Skyping each other, we sexted, and we made each other playlists of our favourite songs on Spotify – all the things teenagers do when they meet someone they like. I learnt that Martyn is a movie lover, and he learnt, with shock, about my terrible lack of movie-going experience. We dove in deep and fast; it felt so natural, so quickly.

In the meantime James was teasing me about the whole thing, calling Martyn my 'Scottish boyfriend', and making childish noises every time I spoke with him. He was extremely supportive, though, never once seeming to have an issue with this relationship I was developing with someone on the other side of the world. About a month after we got back from Scotland, I asked Martyn if he wanted to start properly dating. I wasn't even thinking about the challenges dating someone in Europe would involve, and was oddly surprised when Martyn brought it up. But despite the difficulties of long distance, he said yes. The next day on Facebook I wrote a simple status: 'Massive smile'.

•

After we started 'officially' dating Martyn came to Australia during his holidays, experiencing a Brisbane winter much warmer than the Scottish summer he had left. On the first day we took Martyn on the ferry down the Brisbane River, and I took him on a date to all the bookstores I knew in the city, the two of us leaving little notes in our favourite books for people to read when they bought them. Martyn introduced us to *RuPaul's Drag Race*, and in the space of four weeks we had finished three seasons.

After that trip the relationship felt real, and so I started to tell my family and friends. I got some confused faces, a range of different questions, and some concern from people who thought that I was breaking up with James, but after some chats and explanations, most of the people I really cared about accepted Martyn as my new partner.

The next step was to figure out how to deal with this issue of distance. Martyn immediately expressed a desire to come to Australia, but after having had itchy feet for a while I really wanted to go to Europe. I tried to encourage James to come, but while he theoretically liked the idea, it didn't really work out practically. So we compromised – I would live in Edinburgh for a year and then Martyn would move to Australia.

In Edinburgh Martyn and I figured out what it was like for us to live together, learning lots in the process. We went to the gym together, to movies almost every week, and we managed to travel through a lot of the UK and parts of Europe. I helped Martyn discover the wonders of Berlin, while he took me to one of his favourite cities, Paris. I also discovered that Martyn really likes to keep things very neat, a trait that clashed with my more laissez-faire approach to housework. Soon enough I was learning the proper way to fold shirts, while Martyn learnt to accept a bit of my mess in his bedroom. In the words of Tim Gunn, we made it work.

In the meantime we organised Martyn's move to Australia. He got a working holiday visa and started to put out feelers for a job. We chatted with James about finding a place that would suit the three of us, and spoke about what it would be like to live together. A couple of months after I left Edinburgh, Martyn followed, and now we live in a four-bedroom house in Canberra. James has the room on the ground floor with the en suite, while Martyn has one of the three rooms upstairs, taking the upstairs bathroom as well. We turned the other two rooms into a study for me and a spare bedroom for guests.

Our house is just like any other, really. We do the shopping on Sunday, and divvy out the housework during the week. We've developed a roster of chores that sits on our fridge that includes all our evening plans so we can figure out who will make dinner each night. We watch *RuPaul's Drag Race*, shouting 'Yassssss kweeen' at the top of our lungs, covering up our shame that none of us will ever be as sickening as Sasha Velour, Katya, or Trixie Mattel. Martyn has introduced us to British shows such as *Only Connect* and *The Great British Bake Off*, both of which now form a core part of our viewing.

For our first Christmas as a joint unit we went down to the coast with Martyn's mum Joy, who was visiting from the UK. Just before Joy arrived James got an aggressive stomach bug, one he very kindly shared with me. On the drive back from Sydney airport I had to tell Martyn to pull over so I could throw up in the grass. About half an hour later Martyn hit and killed a kangaroo. The bug then followed us to the coast, with the sound of violent vomiting replacing the peaceful tones of the ocean waves. Welcome to Australia, Joy!

Among all of this normality there are still – at least according to society – some radical ideas: that love does not have to be limited to just one person; that we should be able to enjoy sex and not feel guilty about it; that in fact sex can be healthy, and good fucking fun. And most of all that we can be open and honest about our desires and needs in our relationships, and that we will be all the more healthy for it.

•

After initially telling close friends and family I began to be more confident speaking openly about my new relationship, writing a 'coming out' article for the *Guardian*, posting on Facebook about both James and Martyn being my boyfriends, and being increasingly comfortable showing affection to them both in public places.

In general this has gone very well, but we have received some pushback, and from a group we did not expect – gay men and lesbian women. I've had multiple gays tell me that I'm giving us all a bad name or that I'm giving conservatives ammunition to attack us. One even told me that we have to restrict polyamory as it hurts children – spoken with the same confidence and lack of evidence as conservatives who say the same things about gay parents. We get even more judgement on apps such as Grindr and SCRUFF – dudes on a hook-up app literally having a go at us for being promiscuous and clearly not loving each other enough.

In recent years the gay movement has rammed the idea that 'all love is equal' down everyone's throats (oh, we do love shoving things down each other's throats). But the response to our relationships has shown me that this equality only extends to love that happens between two monogamous gays, behind the closed doors of a bedroom in a moderately sized apartment, with their sex now legitimised by the state. Just take off your wedding rings before the fingering begins.

But here is the crux of this. While infuriating, these arguments are just defence mechanisms against decades of attacks that have told us that gay sex is disgusting, and that it must be stopped immediately. This is how so many of us cope with a dominant narrative that tells us that living in toxically possessive, monogamous, married relationships is the only way we'll ever be properly accepted. This is why gay men continue to judge us about our relationships, attacking us both in private and in public. So even though I hate the arguments, I can't hate the people making them. I know that in a homophobic world it's a way of surviving. But it's a way we should not accept, because the celebration of difference, the celebration of sex and the celebration of all types of love is what makes us strong.

In many ways our relationships are the same as so many others. We do a lot of the same things, have the same fights, enjoy the same small, and large, moments. But our relationships are also very different. They're based on the idea that love does not have to be limited, and that loving one person does not diminish the love you have for another. We go through the same trials and tribulations, but we use different tools to deal with them.

On the first night that James, Martyn and I were properly living together Martyn made us all curry for dinner. James, just home from an interstate work trip and exhausted, missed as he went to put his dinner on the table, smashing his bowl on the table's corner and spraying pinky-orange curry sauce across the white carpet in our rented apartment. The three of us burst out laughing, before quickly scurrying to find whatever cleaning products we had in the house. Our new household had been christened.

Simon Copland

Simon Copland is a PhD candidate in sociology at the Australian National University. He is investigating the rise of the 'new right' in the US and Australia and how these groups engage with questions of identity, gender and sexuality. A freelance writer who has been published in the *Guardian*, *SBS Online Australia*, *BBC Online*, Simon is the co-editor of the online publishing site *Green Agenda*. He also co-produces and presents the podcast *Queers* with Benjamin Riley, a fortnightly discussion of queer politics and culture.

In his free time he likes to powerlift, he loves rugby union, and he's a David Bowie fanatic. Simon is on Facebook **@SimonCoplandWriter**, on Twitter **@SimonCopland** and online at **www.simoncopland.com**.

A SHIT QUEER

Kelly Azizi

jokingly tell my friends that I'm a shit queer. I'm generally perceived to be straight by those who first meet me, and in fact, I make a concerted effort to appear as straight as possible, because I don't feel any compulsion to stand out. Maybe I just don't have the patience for people asking me annoying questions about the tattoos I don't have, the piercings I don't have, the asymmetrical hairdo that I don't have, and every other stereotypical signifier of radical queerness – at least, the radical queerness I've been surrounded by since I came into this aspect of my identity years ago.

My disassociation with this type of fashion aesthetic isn't a judgement. It's just that life is simply easier for me when I appear as a boringly well-presented middle-class person in a world that favours boringly well-presented middle-class white people – especially when you're the daughter of staunchly working-class Lebanese immigrants, and especially when your professional field of interest is dominated by boringly well-presented middle-class white people. To be honest, I like to appear boring. I like the invisibility it affords.

So why should I need to add a disclaimer of sorts to my identity: why do I consider myself a 'shit' queer? After all, I'm politically aware, I'm engaged with queer culture, and it's not like I haven't thought deeply about my own sexuality, or the trajectory that my life took which eventually led me away from heteronormative values into queer identification. How is it that at some point in my routine self-assessment, I ended up ranking myself as 'shit'? As in, the kind of shit that reeks of caged eggs and non-organic meat produce. The kind of shit that's encased in an outfit not-so-proudly brought to you by an affordable yet highly unethical clothing brand that I shall not name (except my shoes, which are apparently 'vegan'). At some point, I went from 'I'm queer and I'm here!' – bolstered by other identity markers that helped me feel empowered and visible, like 'Lebanese-Arab', or 'woman of colour' – to just plain old 'shit'. At some point, I found myself craving *actual* invisibility within a community that kept pointing their finger at me and screaming that my markers of identity are in fact a source of disempowerment and invisibility. I was told that I must always speak up, speak up and defend my politics, even when that other, less glamorous, yet far more pervasive marker of identity – my working-class identity – meant I needed to, well, *work*, just to keep my head above water in a city ruled by property developers and soaring rent prices.

So here I am: feeling shit, overworked, and also tired. Too tired to speak up (at least all the time) in a community that's come to expect a particular response from its 'diverse' constituents. And that's when I realised my story isn't even a story about how I'm a shit queer. It's actually a story about how communities themselves can be shit, and how that shitness will lead communities to inevitable fracture. It's like watching video footage of a car crashing into a wall – *on repeat*. It's a really shit story, because it's repetitious; it follows a formula. But actually, despite how shit that story is, it's also my favourite kind of story, because I see this happen in all communities, and despite the negative connotations of the term 'fracture', there's actually something quite beautiful about that moment of being set free from the community; about that moment when the community sets *itself* free.

These days, it seems like the 'story' (and there isn't just one story) of Sydney's queer community can be traced more easily than ever before: we have social media networks like Facebook and Instagram to thank for that. Community 'discussions' have the potential to become a spectacle in the online realm, to the point that many of us are beyond asking whether our online personas are who we *really* are in real life; we seem to just take it for granted that we are the sum of our Facebook 'status updates' combined. But I do think it's important to differentiate between the realms of online community and real-life community, because so many conflicts within the queer community have taken place with physical distance (which cyberspace conveniently affords) serving as a buffer between the queer bodies actually involved and the real-life consequences suffered by those bodies as a result of those conflicts.

As a younger queer in the mid-2000s, social media was fundamental in determining who was who in the community. The online realm injected into us a sense of real-life cohesion; knowledge of what to do and where to go was literally at our fingertips, and at one point, it seemed like we were all attending the same parties; that we were all friends in real life as much as we were friends on Facebook. The online realm was also fundamental in determining everyone's politics because it gave us the opportunity to excitedly express our opinions across a range of issues both personal and cultural, including gender and sexuality, and race and ethnicity. The public nature of everyone's interactions became key to building up a sense of queer identity on both an individual *and* a collective scale. For a while, it seemed like we all agreed on anything and everything that was deemed progressive and subversive. But eventually the cracks began to show.

Where once the primary purpose of a Facebook status update was to herald marvellous philosophical and political insight on all things queer, it gradually turned into an opportunity to smite those who opposed one's alleged progressive thinking. There was one decisive incident in maybe 2010 involving an evening of queer performance at a historically queer venue in Sydney's Inner West. The performer, a white dancer, drew upon an aesthetic that certain members of the audience perceived as 'tribal'. These audience members then decided that the performer was guilty of culturally misappropriating non-white cultures – although *which* non-white culture the performer was misappropriating no one could really say.

The performer caught wind (via Twitter) that certain audience members were offended, and posted a status update (on Facebook), genuinely wanting to know how and why their performance was racist, so as to avoid the same mistake in future. A massive Facebook blowout ensued, and two parties emerged: the 'anti-cultural-appropriation party' and the 'freedom of artistic expression party'. The former party's belief was that no one – especially white people – had the right to draw upon the culture of ethnicities that they didn't identify with for the purposes of entertainment or creative expression. The latter party's belief was that the former party was an example of political correctness gone too far; that they had no right to police and publicly shame people on the internet; that all creative expression was cultural appropriation on some level; and that the performer was facing unfair criticism because their performance wasn't actually racist; and, besides, the performer was a nice person.

I call this event 'The Great Schism', because really, things were never the same afterwards. Certain players in the online debate suffered social death, or at least fatigue, and went into hiding. I stayed out of the debate, though I watched it unfurl with dismay, not because I was attached to either party's argument: I felt they were both flawed. It was the sheer reductionism of the arguments being thrown about – centred upon ethno-cultural identity, a topic very close to me – all for the sake of satisfying personal vendettas; for satisfying one's sense of self-righteousness.

It was a battle of egos, a clash of ideology in its most methodical and unforgiving state. My initial indifference towards this debate transformed into cold rage when a group of people who I considered friends at the time attempted to draw me into the fray. I was the only non-white queer among them; they spoke with the assumption that I would agree with their arguments, and paid no heed to my silence, which I'd hoped would say a lot during that period of heated outspokenness. I eventually lost my patience and told the most vocal among them to piss off and leave me alone; I asked them if I was a shit person of colour, *a shit queer*, for not agreeing with their views. They quickly apologised, then we disappeared from one another's lives. I've never seen or heard from them since.

Community, hey? For some, it affords amazing support – a familial support – but in my case, too much community is a stranglehold. Since that whole debacle, I've never been able to regard community – any kind of community – as an emotional safety net, as a source of empowerment, or as a reliable guide to morality and ethics. In fact, I loathe using that term 'queer family'; I don't have a queer family, I have good friends, because I already have an extended family in both Australia and Lebanon – and as much as I love my extended family, they're a pain in the arse. In fact, thinking on family as community, I see so many correlations between my experience with queer community and my mother's experience with her once-community: her extended Lebanese family.

My mother, Laudy, who arrived in Australia at the age of fourteen, was always a little different from the rest. She's what I'd call a sassy lady, who flouted conventional ideas of what it meant to be a good Lebanese wife and mother. She was the kind of lady who, in the 1980s, wore tight jeans, electric blue eyeshadow, and sported a glorious perm that glowed artificial burgundy red in the sun. Whenever she visited her husband's family, she stood out among the other women, who adorned themselves in their finest gold jewellery, but who were always dressed in dowdy black clothing because they were mourning some dead relative or other. These other women weren't necessarily content with their lot, but they were *resigned* to being the wives of men, even when their men were dead. Laudy was also the first in the extended family to file for a divorce. Such a thing was unheard of at the time, and relatives near and far tried to intervene, to convince Laudy to go back to her husband, but Laudy told everyone to fuck off.

Laudy's decision to file for divorce was only the beginning of her journey: everything before that – her married life – had been existential stasis. After the divorce, Laudy returned to Lebanon for the first time since departing as a teenager. It was us – her own children – who purchased the plane ticket and gifted it to her for her birthday. She was overwhelmed; it would be the first time she'd see her mother, father and siblings in twenty years. It was an emotional reunion, but one that was fraught with irreconcilable differences. I remember the night when Laudy phoned us in tears. She said, 'Please, one of you, any of you, buy a plane ticket and come here. I want to be with my children. I don't belong here.' It was a shocking revelation. If Laudy didn't belong with the family who raised her, then where did she belong?

Laudy returned to Lebanon several times after that initial visit, but her relationship with her family grew steadily more tense. On one occasion, Laudy's father asked her why she had divorced her husband. She stared her father in the eye and said, 'Well, it turns out I married a man just like you – a man who wants the respect of fatherhood, but none of the responsibility.' Laudy's father didn't say a word. Because, in reality, it wasn't just her husband that Laudy was divorcing; she was divorcing an entire community that had always assumed to know what was best for her; a community whose standards were (unsuccessfully) enforced by Laudy's husband, my father. The divorce signalled the beginning of Laudy's departure from a mode of collective thinking, and into a mode of independent thinking that came with the price of being ostracised.

I recall the one incident that really did it. A relative was to be married to a woman who'd previously been engaged to another man for three years. The family didn't believe this woman was a virgin, and asked to see the bloodstained bed sheets the morning after their wedding night. When Laudy heard about this incident, she lost her shit. She phoned Lebanon and, using colourful Arabic, described what she thought of all those 'fucking assholes who hold their honour between their legs!' By that point, Laudy's family in Lebanon realised that she had gone renegade. Laudy had left her familial community for good, and had decided that her own children – my siblings and I – were all the community she needed.

To this day, Laudy's extended family still can't comprehend her behaviour, and in fact I think they consider her something of a cautionary tale – an example of a shit wife doomed to end up alone in her old age. After all, Laudy isn't the most tactful person, and the truth is that she's gracelessly blundered her way along the path to independence. Which is a beautiful thing, really. Even if Laudy was a shit wife, she's still a brilliant mother who's taught me more about feminism than any feminist theorist ever could.

I wouldn't go so far as to say I've done exactly the same as Laudy – I haven't divorced my community, and I don't intend to. I'm still emotionally and politically invested in my queer identity. I'm also a bit more tactful than Laudy, and I'm privileged to have received the formal education that she never did. But there's no doubt in my mind that Laudy's trajectory has instilled in me an almost brutal desire to break the grain, which is ironic, given that queerness is about breaking the grain of heteronormativity. If I'm breaking the grain of the grain, then what's left for me? Just a big pile of wood pulp; the remnants of a collapsed ideology.

Thinking upon ideology, I recall another incident, where a reputable online news source published an article showcasing Sydney's best queer venues and events. I shared this article on social media, scoffing at the idea that queer identity could be reduced to a list of places where we can all consume 'culture' by spending money. I may have offended a few people who were involved in the article; they perceived my critique as a personal attack. It wasn't meant to be: I just think it's important to contemplate philosophically what it means to be queer; what it means when a supposedly alternative culture becomes accessible to the masses – because I worry that queerness has become more static, more monolithic, more rigidly ideological, and therefore more *marketable*, than it has ever been before. This frightens me, because it's precisely this kind of ideology that silences those who need to be heard the most, the kind of ideology that allows opportunists to profit from a way of life, a cultural politic. This isn't limited to queer identity; this kind of ideology, this kind of marketability, translates to all kinds of communities, whether they are familial, ethno-cultural, creative or queer. You can't really market the Laudys of this world: those misfits who blunder their way through life, playing it by ear as they adapt to a culture that is ever-changing.

Should I feel sad or disappointed that the philosophy of queerness was never as stable as its strongest advocates make it out to be? Not really. 'Queer' was born from the tradition of thinking philosophically about our gendered, sexualised, racialised bodies, and it's in these moments of destabilisation – where communities fracture; where personal philosophies disintegrate and disillusionment ensues – that my body and mind feel the freest. It's in moments of ideological collapse where I can determine my own ways of seeing the world; of seeing my sexuality and ethnicity within that world. With one foot in the community and one foot out of the community, I'm happier being a shit queer, if it means claiming the right to think critically about my own existence. After all, I'm the daughter of Laudy Azizi: shit wife and social misfit.

Kelly Azizi

Kelly Azizi is a writer whose field of interest includes the politics of ethno-cultural identity, the diaspora, and non-white feminism. In 2016, she completed her Master of Cultural Studies degree at the University of Sydney.

Kelly plays an active role in Sydney's art community, and is an advocate for its cultural diversity and inclusiveness. She was the Gallery Administrator at 55 Sydenham Rd – an independent art space in Marrickville – from February 2017 up until its closure in May 2018.

THAT GUY

Nic Holas

One thing I remember about that train ride is the glow of the setting sun filling the carriage, dark lines cut into the amber by the shadows cast by bridges and power lines. In the playback in my mind, the whole carriage is bathed in it.

The memories of that time now are almost distant enough to see myself in them, like a film, as opposed to through my point of view, like some shitty emo music video. That's what happens with distant memories: when we recall them, our minds replay them like films and we see ourselves . . . even though our brains recorded them through our eyes.

It's a Friday evening. One of my last in Melbourne, where I've been living for a few years. On Wednesday, I am flying overseas. To Barcelona, via my childhood home of Kuala Lumpur, and beyond that to Europe, to New York City, and home in time to turn thirty and move away from Melbourne.

I can see the amber light of the sun in the carriage as though it were on a cinema screen, but I can see my phone in my hand as if I am staring at it; recalling it. As if my brain is saying: this is significant. This is a memory that will take hold, not like a hug, more like a blade between your ribs. Painful when it goes in, but even more so when you try to pull it out.

I am in this amber carriage, alert to a sense of things ending and new things beginning. Literally glowing with them. Suddenly, piercing that soft glow of afternoon light is the sharp digital sheen of my phone, activated by an incoming call.

'Dad.'

I stare at it, weighing up my options. It's late, late afternoon. All the delicate amber is draining out of the carriage as the sun continues to set. 'Don't answer a phone call from Dad after dark' is the rule. Plus, I'm on public transport.

I don't want to be that guy.

I've made myself a promise that I've been very good at sticking to: no more answering the phone when Dad calls at night. Increasingly, our conversations have become one-sided, careening murmurs. Foggy monologues stitched together by erratic, haphazard peals of laughter – these days, only from him. I just let him talk and then find a way to excuse myself, then excuse myself again, and again, until through the fog, he gets the hint.

These calls have been going on for a while, ever since my stepmother passed away several months prior. He was grieving. Somewhat stuck in a loop between two of grief's seven stages. A point five stage with a name harder to market than the rest:

'Get tanked on booze, pot, or anything else. Call your only son. Rave about the universe and how you can talk to the moon. Repeat.' My Dad was hurting, and he was living on the Gold Coast, which was far enough away for me not to be able to visit since the funeral. So on the phone, I was patient. Understanding.

I didn't want to be that guy.

Who I was to him was hard to define, though. Dad and I were more like mates than father and son. That's how he saw it. My queerness was never a hurdle; actually, for him it was a source of pride. The youngest of five boys raised in the outer sprawl of post-war Melbourne, Dad was the black sheep of the family. His father, my grandfather, was a rather miserable Scotsman and his mother, my beloved Nan, was a loving and caring woman surrounded by boys.

Of the five boys, only four survived to adulthood and my father was born after the middle son, his elder brother, had passed away in an accident. My Nan never forgave herself, and on the day my young uncle was buried, my grandfather walked into the house and told her she was never to speak of him again.

That's the sort of home my father grew up in, where grief and other powerful emotions were cloaked in a heavy Scottish fog. He had spent his whole life swatting away that fog, but no matter how brightly he shone (and he shone so brightly) my dad would still get lost in it. His early experiments with sex, drugs and rock 'n' roll were his first attempts at an escape from that uptight, suburban world of Melbourne, the rebellions of a young man coming of age in the late sixties and early seventies. Those 'experiments', though, continued through much of my life.

Occasionally, growing up, I could have used a father figure, as opposed to the guy who gave me my first nibble of a pot brownie at age twelve and let me wander around the hippy markets in northern New South Wales, blissfully stoned.

The guy who, a few months later, took me to the Big Day Out in a limo he couldn't afford and let me wander through the sweaty pits of drunk/high adults completely unsupervised while he sat somewhere partying with his girlfriend. I mean, which other twelve year olds can claim to have danced to Itch-E and Scratch-E's 'Sweetness and Light' at the 1995 Gold Coast Big Day Out? It was all pretty fun at the time, but in the face of a seemingly limitless, substance-fuelled parental environment, you kind of want your Dad to make you do your homework.

I wanted him to be that guy.

Back in the train carriage it's a Friday night and he is reaching out. A Friday night: no way that this incoming call wouldn't be laced with booze, pot and whatever else. No way it would be brief. No way I want to take that call while I'm sitting on a train.

So the phone goes unanswered. 'I'll ring him back tomorrow,' I think.

Maybe I don't think that; maybe I just roll my eyes at the increasing difficulty of being his son.

Maybe I wonder when he is going to stop living like this.

Moments later, the sun has set and I am ascending the escalators of a city mall, carrying me to the cinema where my friend is waiting to meet me. My phone starts to buzz once more.

Unlike my amber train carriage, in the neon lightstorm of the shopping centre my phone's digital flashes fit right in.

This time though, it isn't my Dad. It's my sister.

Between the hustle and hum of a thousand or so people chatting, shopping and commuting, it is tricky to make out what she is saying. Her naturally husky voice is even harder than usual to understand, punctuated by panicked sobs.

'Dad [sob] . . . is [sob] . . . trying [sob] . . . to [sob] . . . kill [sob] . . . himself.'

It's weird, getting life-changing news on the way to, or in the middle of, a relatively banal event. My first thought is, 'I can still go to the movies; I don't want to cancel on my friend.' Memories may be distorted, but your brain in crisis is bizarre.

Suddenly, as people around me are buying their popcorn, I am trying to piece together what has happened – or, as it turns out, is happening: unfolding somewhere in real time, as we were talking on the phone. A DVD commentary on someone else's cinematic memory. Dad's final one, if everything went to plan.

DVD commentary is going to be something we explain with embarrassment to young people when we are old. What a bizarre, late-capitalism value add that was . . . and it's over now. Even weirder. You see, even in writing about this, years later, I attempt to distract from the pointy end of the story, the hard-to-remember bits. But I press on, as the detailed parts of the memories, pointless as they may be, start to fog and fade.

So there we are, my little sister and I, wondering if this is it. She had also missed his call, probably for the same reasons

I had. But unlike me, she listened to his voicemail not long after he left it.

She heard another foggy monologue, but this time not peppered with any one-sided laughter, just a small voice, tight in the throat. Sad and unhinged. Saying goodbye.

My sister panicked, and called him. He answered, but was unintelligible and hung up not long after. Now he wasn't answering, his phone going straight to voicemail. And she was spiralling through the terrifying notion that she had just heard Dad's voice for the last time.

This wasn't my first time being told that my Dad was trying to commit suicide. But it was hers. My little sister with the big heart, who had grown up repeatedly being told she was 'just like Dad'.

Amidst the panic and the sobs, she wants his address. She had called 000, but she doesn't know where he actually lives . . . and neither do I. Dad had been asked to move out of his partner's apartment by her family not long after she passed away. He is living with a mate, somewhere on the glamorously ugly part of the Gold Coast. That's all I know, and knowing the Gold Coast, that doesn't exactly narrow it down.

We hang up, so as to not tie up the phone line and so I can try to find his address.

I call him (maybe he'd pick up for me, his best mate). Straight to voicemail. I leave him one. He might never hear it, but if he does, he might be able to hear what I am trying to tell him.

So I listen to the voicemail my Dad left me after I ignored his call. Just like the one he left my sister. I can't recall a word of what he said, but I could hear what he was trying to tell me. He was sorry.

Through my uncle, we track down Dad's address and send the police and ambulance. They had to break in to the house.

Dad had taken a lethal amount of the OxyContin my stepmother had been prescribed to help relieve the pain from her terminal cancer.

But unlike her, Dad didn't die. He was in hospital, and he was going to be ok. Sort of. But he didn't die.

Later that night, it is my turn to break down, on the phone to my mother as I relay the evening's events. That memory is one I can see myself in. Standing by my closed bedroom door in my share house. Through the sobs, anger.

'I wish he had just done it. I wish he'd just followed through on something, for once.'

A couple of days later, as soon as I can, I am on a plane to the Gold Coast. In a humble little room, a humble man lay beside a humble view of nothing in particular. It was a cold, rainy day in the city that promises endless summer vacations. Going to school there, I knew how broken that promise was.

Dad is as relieved to see me as he is ashamed. I am angry with him right up until the moment I round the corner and enter his hospital room. Where does empathy go, when you come face to face with the man who brought you into the world, but wanted to leave you in it without him? Leave you to deal with the wound he'd inflict, because his suffering was all consuming?

There is a moment waiting for all of us when we realise we are charged with the responsibility of taking care of our parents.

For me, that moment involved pushing my anger and hurt to one side to show Dad patience and kindness. It was getting in a cab and going to his house, rummaging through his room and finding all of my dead stepmother's leftover painkillers and flushing them down the toilet. It was putting all that hurt and anger someplace else, at least for a moment.

I didn't want to be that guy.

I don't change my holiday plans. I'm not sure what I was trying to prove, what sort of message I thought I was sending him. Something along the lines of 'Your behaviour will not be rewarded. My life will go on.'

So a few days later, I am on that plane heading to Europe. Distract. Displace. Distort. In the sweaty streets of Barcelona, Lisbon, Paris, New York City, on apps and dancefloors and in sex clubs, I prove to anyone and everyone just how much life I have in me. A recent pattern of behaviour becomes all consuming, and I allow an endless cavalcade of men inside me, with literal gay abandon. They fill me up. One of them, it turns out, with HIV.

It isn't his fault.

It isn't my Dad's fault.

It isn't anyone's fault.

I am just . . . that guy.

'That guy' goes on to play a big role in changing the way we talk about HIV in this country, and that wouldn't have happened without that moment in my life taking me where it did. I learnt that we can't hold on too tightly to what we're supposed to be, what the world expects of us.

My father crumbled beneath the weight of expectation, so often trying to make his way out of the fog. The weight of expectation placed on queer men to avoid contracting HIV means that when you do make that mistake, you too can crumble. I've now seen many people whose lives are forever made foggy by their diagnosis. For a while, I threw myself into helping them, all the while refusing to help or forgive Dad.

You might think it's a little shitty to write so plainly about someone else's suffering, but suicide is an act that puts one person out of their pain and leaves it for their loved ones to trip over, again and again. When it's your father doing that to you, it makes you feel a little shitty.

But years later, Dad and I laugh together again, and we laugh often. There are no more foggy monologues. He has stopped drinking, but not stopped living. That works for him; it works for us. For our friendship, and as father and son.

Once I became HIV-positive I could see very clearly a long line of male elders stretching back through time, many of them taken early by unfair circumstances. I welcomed into my life new male role models, survivors of the gay plague, uncles and daddies. Some of them I went to bed with; some took me under their wing and helped me become the activist I am today.

I have had many daddies, but only one father. Like my HIV elders, I am grateful that he stuck around.

Nic Holas

Nic Holas is an activist, writer, and co-founder of The Institute of Many (TIM), Australia's largest grassroots movement for People Living with HIV. Nic's writing on HIV/AIDS, LGBTIQA+ issues, human rights and pop culture has appeared in *Archer,* the *Guardian, Sydney Morning Herald, SBS, Hello Mr., The Lifted Brow,* and *Junkee,* as well as in international and local queer media.

Nic has been a frequent guest on current affairs TV and radio, including appearances on *Q&A, Lateline, Radio National,* and *triple j.* For the last 15 years Nic has also worked nationally and internationally as a director, performance maker, performer and producer.

ONE METRE SQUARE

Peter Polites

Greek lesbians do the best *zeibekiko*. I learnt this in my twenties when I went to the Greek and Gay Group. GAGG. I also learnt Greek gay men are just as gross as Straight Bros. Whenever a new person would walk in, they chanted like a chorus 'Welcome to GAGG!' and after saying the acronym they would make a choking sound.

The meetings were always held after work hours and started in the dark. They were never signposted; there was an unacknowledged secrecy around them. To be discreet, people going to the meeting would park their cars down the street from the community centre. After the meetings, when we were full of *mezedes,* participants walked straight to their cars, even though we could have talked till sunrise. Going to GAGG reminded me of an old nursery rhyme my mum used to sing to me. In it, children would ask the moon to show them the way to school. The nursery rhyme was a few hundred years old; its lyrics originated during the Ottoman occupation and the song was a memory of a time when children used to go to school at night to learn their language. The reason they went at night is because learning Greek was banned under penalty of death.

I used to look up to the moon to show me the way to GAGG and at the time I was searching for my own personal hoplite slash soccer player, but GAGG was frequented by lesbians and gay men in their thirties who still lived at their parents' homes. The umbilical cord will always strangle the Greek children of the diaspora and the meetings always descended into what looked like shouting matches but were just talking. Even though we were different from our hetero-parental units, we still managed to maintain what outsiders would call stereotypes, and insiders would call traditions.

I didn't find a hoplite slash soccer player. I did meet a young lesbian who grew up a few streets away from me. She had been quietly coming to the meetings, sitting in the corner and occasionally filling up her paper cup with instant coffee from the samovar. Her parents called her Soula but she introduced herself as Tas. She had fine white skin, the deepest blue eyes and a button nose. Her features were emphasised with a pageboy haircut that swept over the left side of her face. When Tas spoke, her vowels dropped three octaves and the consonants frizzled at the end. Although she had the delicate features of a pretty Albanian refugee, her voice had the timbre and pronunciation of a bro who drinks two protein shakes while getting a sleeve tattoo in one session.

At one meeting, when the moon outside was in a shape of a crescent, the shouting turned into dancing. All the gay men did the *tsifteteli*. We shook our hips and flicked our wrists in the air. When we became tired we played the slower songs of the *zeibekiko*. Tas got up off the chair and walked into the middle of the room. She mapped out the one metre square she would be dancing in with her foot. The rest of us surrounded her; some got on our knees and started clapping to the rhythm. She put her foot down with mourning, her hips were lonely and her body and its problems stayed anchored to the ground. Her arms extended out like the wings of an eagle, her soul trying to break free from the circular and limited movements.

The *zeibekiko* is about mourning and loneliness and only done by men but as Tas expressed her steps, we felt it, we felt her and she danced as us.

I asked her out on a friend date and we met at the Corinthian restaurant, which had been run by the same Greek family for the last thirty years. The Corinthian was there during Greek youth gang wars, when the streets were littered with bloody knives and exploded *yeeros*. In the eighties when graffiti on bridges claimed that Cops Killed Tasos, it opened every midday, serving its casserole green beans with dill.

We sat down at the table and each table had a candle covered in glass that scattered dots of light over the cloth. There were heavy arches that rose up the walls and curled over the ceiling; they had stucco on them to give the effect of blunt stalactites. They gave the place the feel of a cave.

We ate and Tas told me stories. When Tas was a teenager she walked into the kitchen with a new boy-short haircut, and neither parent said anything. They heaped more green beans on her plate and they ate as a family. Once, when going to a cousin's christening at the church, Tas wore pants and a collared shirt. Her mother looked her up and down and gave her the car keys.

Floating around their interactions were thought bubbles of expectation – expectations that she would take care of them into old age, pushing them in wheelchairs down church aisles.

She fessed up her story. Her voice increased in decibels and sharpened like iron bolts. Her big eyes opened up more and her palm extended flat and hard as it chopped invisible bits of the air. Her voice was directed at me and for a second I looked around to see if it was reverbing onto any of the customers. The other Greeks didn't notice. They chopped the air just as much as she did and I realised what I took for vibrancy was just people talking loudly.

I used my fork to scrape mince from the bottom of my plate and I asked Tas if she was ready to give up her own life to save theirs. It wasn't giving up life, she said. It was just compromise.

Tas told me the ritual that she undertook to put her mum's wheelchair in the car. Rolling her next to the open passenger door, sliding her feet off, her mum holding onto the car door as she swirled her body to the seat. Tas took her to the Greek church on Sunday, finding parking and rolling her mum up the side ramp. She stood next to her mum while old men sang ancient hymns. When the priest went off topic and said that women wearing pants were poisoning society, old women with their heads covered in black scarves turned to look at Tas. When the priest went off topic and went on a rant against the homosexual influence in the Australian community, Tas stood stoically behind her mother's wheelchair and took a deep breath. Weren't you affected, I asked Tas? I felt bad, but only for the priest's gay son, she said.

I told Tas I needed a cigarette after the meal. I went outside onto Illawarra Road and a dry, vicious wind ran through me. All the shops had closed and the streets were empty. I stood close to the road and mapped out where I would smoke with my foot. I traced out one metre square, with the tips of my shoes scraping across asphalt. Around me cars crawled along the street and doors slammed shut like people clapping. I swayed to the wind. I moved the cigarette to my mouth in a repetitive gesture, up and down. I exhaled the blue smoke and it rose all the way up to the moon. The ember reached the fibrous bud and I flicked it onto the ground; the sole of my foot stepped heavily on the pavement to extinguish it and I extended both my arms up as I spun around slowly to re-enter the Corinthian.

Peter Polites

Peter Polites is a writer of Greek descent from Western Sydney. He is a member of the Western Sydney CaLD literary and activist collective SWEATSHOP. He has written performance texts for Urban Theatre Projects and been published in *Overland*, *Meanjin*, *The Big Black Thing* and *The Lifted Brow*. His first novel is called *Down the Hume* – it is a queer noir.

MAKING HOME (TO ALL THE LESBIANS I'VE LOVED BEFORE)

Quinn Eades

I am in Aotearoa for Same Same But Different, Auckland's queer writers festival. I arrived three days early to see my sister, who has moved here from Hong Kong to make a home with her husband and two children, one of whom I've never met. Born as I was leaving a 16-year lesbian relationship and coming out as trans, there is a small person now, a niblet of mine in the world, who I may never meet. I sent my sister messages to say I was coming, to say I'd love to see her and the kids. I could see that she'd read them (the double tick in WhatsApp) but there was no reply. On a greenhot Christmas afternoon last year, I sent a final text:

Merry Xmas. Hope you had a great day. Sounds like you don't want to see me in Auckland. If you ever want to talk or reconnect I'm here.

⩗

Read, but no reply. How long does a person wait for a loved one, a sister, to respond? This sister of mine who curled into me after nightmares, whose hair I braided before school. She loved her long, thin, blonde hair but cried whenever it was brushed. There were threats from my mother, too tired for a morning fight – 'I'll cut it off if you can't brush it' – so I did it. Quietly, gently, in our bedroom. Learnt how to hook her hair into the crooks of my little fingers so I could turn the hanks into plaits. She didn't cry with me. Now I do it for one of my boy children, who is overwhelmed in the world often and uses his hair as a screen, a sensory blocker, sunglasses; as a space between him and the brightloudhot day. This sister of mine who emblazons herself with quiet diamantés – you have to get close to see them, embedded in lip gloss, along the sides of her glasses, on the buckles of her shoes. Read, but no reply.

Read, but no reply. How long does a person wait? For the rest of a life, I think. I am in Auckland days early, so instead of seeing my heartlove second-born diamanté-sparkled sister, I stay with an old friend of my boyfriend's. Anne is a 78er, a lesbian who marched from Taylor Square to Kings Cross alongside many others on a wintry night in Darlinghurst. Meant to be a celebration, the march ended with more than fifty arrests, bashings and abuse (mostly perpetrated by the police).

Tall, blonde, spouting stories, making me spit my tea with laughter on the back deck with cicadas and cigarette smoke and stars. We talk about our lives. We draw a chart in the dark air, of all of the ways we connect (one degree of separation).

We talk about lesbians. Why? Because my mum is a lesbian and Anne is about the same age as her. Because I came out to my mum as a lesbian at twelve. Because before I began this particular becoming (transmasc person and parent, queer, bent), I was a lesbian, although I preferred to call myself a dyke, for the strength of this word on my tongue and the way it caused discomfort in others. Because this word, lesbian, has become a gloss for transphobic, limited, judgemental and narrow among some queer and trans folk.

Anne lives with Verity and Lisa, who run Garnet Station, the café next door. Rainbow flags flying, a community gathering place with strong coffee and a singing cowboy for kids twice a week. When I eat their spanakopita it is a green salt burst in the mouth. Everyone knows everyone else. So many hellos. Attached to the café is a tiny theatre, and the night I arrive there is a show on in the forty-seat space, whose walls are covered with lesbian art. 'I'm not a lesbian but my girlfriend is.' I take a picture of this framed text, and send it to my girlfriend back in Melbourne.

The show begins with an older dyke called Hills singing rough and sweet to strummed acoustic guitar. I know this. I know this. I have been in more rooms with singing dykes playing guitars than I can count. I have been one of those dykes singing and strumming a guitar with calloused fingertips and a crack in my voice ('Closer to Fine', 'The Queen and the Soldier', 'Zombie'). Andrea makes a grand entrance through two black curtains at the back of the stage, flinging them behind her and thrusting her black-clothed body through, and everybody cheers. She is known and loved here. Over the next hour she sings, mimes and performs her story, which is a story of babies born young, addiction, studying mime in France, rape and sexual assault, mothers and grandmothers, and love. At the end we cheer and hoot, and Andrea and Hills grin wide and thrilled at the response.

I think about my lesbian heritage. Running wild at women's dances in the eighties. Knowing all the words to the Topp Twins' 'Untouchable Girls' ('We're stroppy, we're aggressive, we'll take over the world'), and my little sister and I doing Lynda and Jools impersonations on an iron-laced balcony in Balmain, topless lesbians everywhere, breasts brown-globed and drooping in the Sydney sun. I was always Jools, with an elastic-waisted skirt pulled on over my jeans. The Topp Twins were there among the topless lesbians, laughing their heads off at our parody.

Dancing my little kid heart out to the Party Girls and the Stray Dags. Eighties bands full of women. Watching them smash out drum beats and turn up their electric guitars. The lead singer of the Stray Dags was Mystery Carnage and I thought it was the coolest name in the whole wide world. All of us in gym boots and fluorescent socks. Painting banners for peace marches, land rights marches, Anzac Day protests. Black Deaths in Custody meetings in our lime-green kitchen. Eating my mother's home-made toasted muesli (the smell of honey and oats when it baked). Being the only kids at school with Vogel's bread, a packet of sultanas or a piece of dried pineapple our sugary treat, and watching envy-eyed the kids who popped open small packets of crisps. Being told girls can do anything. Over and over and over again. Learning strength, learning fight, learning love.

I will keep building this particular lesbian utopia, but know that this story on its own is an untruth. There were crushing abandonments. Screaming. Fights that tore at our insides. Exhaustion. Fear. Addiction. There are always these stories weaving in among rallies and the fluorescent fabric paint we used to decorate our own T-shirts and sneakers, and I have written many of them. But I remind myself that we remember too easily what is painful about a moment; that we unremember too quickly those glittering threads of joy. That we need to tell the golden moments as well – there is always both/and. Utopias can't exist without dystopias, as well as what runs in between.

What runs in between: my mum no longer coping. The share houses she tried to parent us in – and the dream of a feminist lesbian village – falling apart. Undiagnosed bipolar. Cutting. Blood like red paint. Protest posters on the walls ('You are standing on Aboriginal land'), a three-storey bunk hand-built by the women we lived with. Brigette filling our Santa sacks (always with 'Ms Claus' written on their outsides) with shoplifted art supplies and wooden toys. My sister and I being sent to Katoomba to live with our grandmother. We sobbed all the way up the mountain. My mum made us books, those A5 black-covered ones with the red corners and lined pages, so we could draw pictures in them for her. Five and three. So small. Drawing the Skyway and the Scenic Railway with desperately bright colours. Learning how to dress for the cold.

Coming home, back down the mountain, to a house on Mary Street in Leichhardt because my mum had fallen in love and was feeling better. Her front room with its bay windows, an old jam jar full of her home-made patchouli oil scenting the whole place, a frangipani tree in the front garden. Backyard with a tyre swing, swimming pool at the end of the street, wooden climbing frame inside the house, on the bottom floor. A shared bedroom that was so big we could practice our gymnastics and dance routines in there. Being given rollerskates, those ones with a key to make them longer or shorter, that strapped on over our hand-decorated Dunlop Volleys. Dancing to Cyndi Lauper, Culture Club and Split Enz in the lounge room. My mum's girlfriend filling the house with people, rolling joints on album covers, pulling out her guitar and playing Patsy Cline's 'Don't Fence Me In'. One year for her birthday we made her a song-book and filled it with her favourite songs, carefully notating the chords, adding stickers, making borders with purple and green pencils.

My mum not good again. Her best friend giving me *The Lion, The Witch and The Wardrobe*. Discovering I could disappear completely inside books (not hearing, not feeling the chair underneath my eight-year-old legs). Sobbing when Aslan died. Writing my first poems. Being told, again, that girls can do anything.

She was astonishingly good at birthdays. Her poet father shot himself in the head when she was fifteen. His death was a schism, a trauma so big she was gaping open and couldn't manage much of the time, but she made up for it on our birthdays. One year she saved and saved so she could give me a set of seventy-two Derwent pencils; when I opened the slim metal box they unfolded in two decks. I loved them so much I refused to sharpen them. I opened the cold box one morning and found an olive green pencil that was two-thirds the length of the rest, realised my sister had used and sharpened it, and cried for hours.

On my eleventh birthday it was raining so we had a barbecue on the tiny balcony of our Glebe flat. The lesbians who lived in the flat downstairs and diagonally opposite (who taught us to tap dance; who set up a tightrope in the back yard for us; who taught us to tumble, be strong, take risks) came up and joined in. I had a plaited rat's tail that was 15 centimetres long and blue spray-painted hair. My favourite present that year came from my mum – a white T-shirt covered in hot pink naked women's bodies.

I told her I thought I was a lesbian when I was twelve, and still remember her saying, 'Maybe you should try boys first, when you're ready, so you know.' Her worry that I was following what was around me, rather than finding my own way.

Her writing. The way she kept trying to complete a half-finished Masters in Writing at the University of Technology but took an editing job instead because more than anything else she didn't want to be on a single parent's pension for the rest of her life. Knowing that one of her lecturers, Drusilla Modjeska, thought she would be part of the next generation of feminist Australian writers, and spending her time editing annual reports instead of making a writing world for herself because kids; because the village hadn't worked; because her ghost-poet father was always there, a smear at the corner of her eye, a gun shot echo every afternoon.

All the other lesbians who looked after us when my mum couldn't: ex-girlfriends and ex-friends who took us to circus workshops, drove us to dance lessons, gave me a flute so I would have an instrument to play – I had orchestral dreams. Untreated bipolar made it hard to keep relationships going, and in the eighties the lack of education and understanding about mental health issues meant she was often isolated and ostracised. They tried to look after her, but couldn't, so they looked after me and my sister instead. All those women's dances, often at the Balmain Town Hall. Bra-less dykes dancing to Eurythmics covers and falling in love with Deborah Conway. A drinks table full of plastic cups. Every second woman in purple and green.

At one of those dances my mum had drunk a lot of champagne. My sister and I danced and ran, loose and fast, across the thumping wooden floor. We kept trying to find her; each time we did, she was in a different dark corner. Each time we did, she turned and walked away, champagne glass in one hand, rollie in the other. I know what this feels like now because I am a parent too, and sometimes when I'm being climbed on and whinged at the only thing I can do is to walk the other way and breathe. We persisted, and so did she. Eventually a friend of hers noticed what was happening, and took us to the drinks table for a lemonade.

'How about you girls stay at my place tonight?' she asked. 'I've already checked with your mum and she says it's okay.' We found her one more time, near the front of the stage, and said goodbye. She could barely look at us, her smile a tight grimace. Her friend tucked us under each of her arms and drove us to her house in Petersham. Streetlight flashes through the back windows, the sticky vinyl bucket seats, holding my sister's hand on the drive.

We stumble-followed her through a pitch black Sydney garden, through the back door propped open with a brick, and into her bed. I don't remember where she slept, or what the morning was like. I do remember feeling scared about the door being propped open with a brick, that a stranger could have gotten into her house. The thick wet scrape across concrete as she pulled the door wider so we could all get through. I do remember the smell of an unfamiliar bed. I don't remember how we got home.

When I was twelve I started visiting one of my mum's ex-girlfriends at her little house in Glebe by myself. A blue Sydney bus would take me to her home, a place that smelled of dope and sandalwood incense. She was the first person to show me the Serenity Prayer, and it was my mantra for many hard years. One afternoon we were looking through the back pages of the *Sydney Morning Herald* and I spotted a tiny square of text that said Pact Youth Theatre was looking for thirteen to eighteen year olds to join. She made the call for me, lied and said I was thirteen, got the address and took me in one Saturday morning.

Falling down building at the bottom of George Street. Dusty floorboards and old curtains. Ten other kids who became my friends. Adults who kept a quiet eye out for me. I learnt some mime there. I heard Peter Gabriel and Kate Bush sing 'Don't Give Up' there, and was heartbroken and full of love at exactly the same time. One of the adults played that song over and over again, while we stood scattered through the space, purple velvet fabric making a cloak for each of us, learning how to open and then close the cloak so slowly that it would take the whole song. Sunlight striking us at odd angles through the broken roof, those keening voices, wrapped in purple velvet, learning muscle control, learning strength, learning time, learning body, learning self.

So in the tiny theatre next door to the lesbian-run café in Auckland, surrounded by lesbians and queers, hearing guitar strum and a life story made in a fire of sex, theatre, drugs and alcohol, activism and lesbian love, I know I'm in my home-place. I remember with my body being loved by all those women. I remind myself that it was there, on the grass, in women's dances, at protest marches, at birthday parties, on circus mats, in a George Street warehouse, that I learnt how to be strong, how to fight, how to open, how to rally. It is because of those many strong women's arms and voices that I got enough to survive my own becoming. To be here, without my sister, among friends of friends, tracing my own queer map on a light-strung back deck. Being open. Keeping strong. Making home.

Quinn Eades

Quinn Eades is a Tracey Banivanua Mar Research Fellow and Lecturer in Interdisciplinary Studies at La Trobe University. A writer, researcher, gutter philosopher and poet, his book *Rallying* was awarded the 2018

Mary Gilmore Award for best first book of poetry. Quinn is the author of *all the beginnings: a queer autobiography of the body*, and he recently published a co-edited volume of life-writing, poetry, and scholarship titled *Offshoot: Contemporary Life Writing Methodologies and Practice*. When he's not working, Quinn is hanging with his kids, cuddling his pups, and watching reruns of *The Unbreakable Kimmy Schmidt* or drag makeup tutorials on YouTube.

GOING THE DISTANCE

Nayuka Gorrie

I am in love and my heart is full. Women in my family don't have that kind of love. That sort of forever love. Most women in my life fuck some fulla and at some point are just like 'Ah fuck it, you'll do' and after a few weeks together they move in. Blackfullas call this 'married up' but in the queer community we would call it 'lesbianism'.

I have the sort of love that makes my heart burst and write bad poetry and if I could draw I would sketch tasteful nudes that dinner guests are awkwardly forced to engage with and compliment me on. If you had met me three years ago you would think I was a bit of a different person. I was in a relationship with a cishet man and contemplating whether I was asexual or maybe a lesbian. I'm neither by the way but the mind goes places. I hated PDA. Straight couples grossed me out even though I was in one.

Now I happily proclaim to thousands of strangers how hot my boyfriend is and how they would make a great parent and blah blah blah, are you bored yet? I know it's boring but I also believe it's resistance. In 2017, our community went through months of state-sanctioned hate and people telling us our relationships aren't valid so if straight people find my public displays of ridiculous love annoying, they can just shut up and deal with it.

Last year, Witt and I went to Japan. It was as beautiful and idyllic as you would imagine a queer, vegan holiday to be. We drank a lot of beer and flavoured alcoholic beverages. We ate very well. I had one of the best days of my life there. We hired bikes in Kyoto and rode around and got drunk and Witt just looked perfect and the weather was perfect. It was perfect.

But the trip wasn't all sunshine and rainbow flag emojis. On the trip, we had a kidnapping scare. Adult napping. Human thievery. Whatever it's called, it was my worst nightmare.

You see, when I was young, maybe like four or five, I caught a bus with my mum from Victoria to Queensland. At one of the stops, Mum got off the bus to have a smoke and the bus left without her and I ended up pissing my pants and crying at the back of the bus, so I probably have some attachment issues, but who doesn't? My mum also used to be a cop and occasionally would get hurt on the job. I have grown to hate cops and I've also learnt to assume the worst.

Witt and I caught a lot of trains in Japan. I know it's really hard to imagine if you live in Australia, kind of like imagining a world without capitalism or a stable federal government, but trains in Japan just make sense; they are quick, frequent and on time. On the train, we would get drunk and eat soba noodles and other snacks. The Japanese are great at snacks.

Witt is really daring and cheeky, which is normally a delightful quality. We thought we had become seasoned at trains. Tipsy off the cheap beers, Witt would quickly duck off the train when it stopped at small towns and they would go get us more snacks or more beer. Predictably, I would panic every time they left because of my aforementioned fear of being left behind on transport. So, in this instance, I told Witt our plan; I always have a plan. 'Plan for the worst but expect the best,' I always say. The plan was, if for some reason the train did just leave without them, we would meet back at the departure point.

We were leaving Hiroshima. We rocked up to the train station and saw a train, seemingly our train, leaving for Osaka, waiting on the right track. There was about eleven minutes to spare, enough time to at least get some beer and snacks. Witt told me to wait on the train: I had everything, their wallet, their phone, their passport and all of our luggage. About a minute after they left, though, the train doors closed and the train sped off. My worst nightmare was realised. As the train was moving I started quietly saying 'no'. Eventually those 'no's turned into a quiet shout. 'No, no, *no*, NO, NO!' The Japanese are so polite they just ignored me.

As per the plan, I got off at the next station and got the first train back to Hiroshima. I tried not to freak out too much because I thought there was still a really good chance Witt was there. But when I got back to Hiroshima, they were not there. Initially, I thought perhaps we were at different parts of the station so I looked everywhere. I thought maybe they were looking for me at another part of the station. But they simply weren't there. I waited until the last train but I still couldn't find them. Sobbing, I finally spoke to the staff, who looked at me like I was some weird parasite.

My mind truly went places. In all of my hysteria, though, there was one place I avoided – the police. Witt is an abolitionist and even if they did run into any problems the police are the last people they would be inclined to go to for assistance, and rightly so. Sidenote – I had three separate dealings with police in Japan. It's comforting to know that it doesn't matter where you are in the world, you will be overpoliced. A nice little slice of home.

I circled around the police station. I resisted the urge to go in until I couldn't resist it anymore. Then I went in and started crying, saying my boyfriend was missing. At this point I thought Witt had been kidnapped by some weird Japanese sex slave cartel. I imagined myself as some kind of hotter, younger and blacker Liam Neeson in the film *Taken* starring Liam Neeson. I wondered, 'Will I have to stay in Japan until I find my boyfriend? Would I have to post "Missing" posters? "Missing: Hot White Twink last seen at Hiroshima Station".'

The police asked me all these questions. I felt really guilty: what if they spoke to the police at the Osaka station and then the police just grabbed Witt – how would they react? Police as a principle don't like queers. What if they got arrested? Would

I have to sue the police? How do I take the police to court? What had I done?

So, here I was stressing, thinking I had either lost them to a cartel or the police, which is pretty much the same thing I guess. I was not a hot young black Liam Neeson. I was a little baby who would never see her boyfriend again and would die in Hiroshima mistaking every hot twink for her boyfriend. Would I settle down and find a Japanese partner? Would they support my quest to find my boyfriend? How much would it cost to photocopy pictures of Witt? What hashtag would I use to start the campaign? What photo would I use?

I called my brother, sobbing. I don't even know what time it was in Australia. He told me everything was going to be okay.

But the police were useless, to be completely honest. They laughed at me when they realised I had Witt's phone, because how was I going to contact them if I had their phone – LOL. I get that, cops – that's why I'm here in this rundown train station police station and not already sexting them at a hotel right now. Just do your job.

I waited at the station while the police called other stations. I waited and waited until miraculously Witt came online. They were alive!

I messaged them. They had gotten the train to Osaka and thought I would just meet them there. They didn't remember the plan. I ended up staying at a cheap hotel then caught the first train out of Hiroshima. When I saw them at Osaka station I squeezed them so hard and cried with relief.

Hold your twinks tight tonight. Hold your twinks tight.

Nayuka Gorrie

Nayuka Gorrie is a Kurnai/Gunai, Gunditjmara, Wiradjuri and Yorta Yorta freelance writer who has written for *The Guardian*, *Junkee*, *Vice*, *SBS* and others. She also writes for TV, most notably for ABC TV's *Black Comedy*.

GOTTA MAKE WAY FOR THE HOMO SUPERIOR
A SHORT TALE ABOUT HEROES, COCK AND CANCER

Vicki Melson

The seventies were not an easy decade for me. I was a fucking ugly kid. Almost 6 feet tall at twelve years old, stick thin, flat-chested, with braces on my wonky British teef, and somehow, to the horror of my racist parents, an afro, which my mother parted in the middle and attempted to smooth down, causing two permanent triangles to form on my head.

I used to write letters to God, who none of us believed in, begging him to cut off my legs and make me normal like the other girls. My mother found these notes and squirrelled them away with all my other secrets. So many secrets. In the supermarket, they called me Sonny. I wanted to die.

And then punk came along and saved my skinny arse. Suddenly it was ok not to look like Farrah Fawcett-Majors, and being a freak was cool. I found myself a relatable heroine. Her name was Poly Styrene, the lead singer of X-Ray Spex, a mixed-race girl with a mouth full of metal, outrageous dress sense and a wavering, fierce voice. She made my world turn day-glo.

After school, I'd sneak off to the park on my cheap skateboard with its terrible roller-skate wheels and change my outfit in the bushes. Sometimes I would simply put a torn bin liner over my clothes, adorned with safety pins. Other days, an oversized shirt that I'd stolen from my father, ripped to shreds and covered in ink. Quink ink, from the bottle that I used to fill up my school fountain pen. Rebellion at its best.

Pinned to my flat chest was a large Snoopy badge that read 'Punk'. He had a safety pin through his nose and wore chains. Hot older punks would always comment on that badge. I still have it. Thanks, Snoopy.

I still wasn't quite sure what to do with this new version of me. I had no self-esteem, and my racist parents were also homophobes, so I spent my entire childhood as an outsider in my own home, thanks to being born with the burning knowledge that I was neither of those things and would fight my whole fucking life to defend that. Thankfully, I had someone on my side: my maternal grandmother, who liked to call herself Dolly. I call her Nana B and she sits on my shoulder and keeps me company to this day.

My nana loved me hard. I could do no wrong. In her eyes, I was beautiful, courageous, funny and talented. She loved my zest for life and championed all the things in me that my father tried so hard to snuff out. She loved my rebellious, questioning nature; she adored my quirkiness and my irrepressible, highly irritating hyperactivity. She openly favoured me above all others, viciously batting away the other grandchildren. I loved every second with her.

Nana B was a true wonder. Swathed in fake Pucci blouses paired with trouser suits, and reeking of Chanel No. 5, she worked through husbands like a trouper. She ran a guesthouse. Three storeys of tiny rooms filled with smelly, lonely, elderly men who would defend her with their lives. She kept their rent money in a tin and diddled the taxman. They boiled eggs in their kettles and made tea with the water.

Her own floor of the house was a seventies palace filled with lava lamps, swivel chairs and Laura the Afghan hound who sat on the rug surrounded by cauldrons of homemade wine, which bubbled on the radiators nearby. She had an enormous colour television that also swivelled. Swivelling was the height of fashion. We weren't allowed a colour television in our house because my father said they were too dangerous.

Unlike my teetotaller parents, Nana B loved a drink and loaded the sherry trifle up at Christmas so we'd all unwittingly get pissed. She also loved punk and would demand that my friends and I come over to give her fashion shows, where she'd serve us prawn cocktail crisps and Coca-Cola. We loved her.

Being the rebel that she was, when Nana B got sick, she refused to take her medication, aged a hundred years overnight and died. Her last few days were spent wearing my clothes. At the time I found this odd. Now I find it beautifully comforting.

On my last visit to her, she asked me not to let her die. I said I wouldn't, and then she did, and I broke inside.

So I did what all broken kids do. I searched for validation in any possible way and I found it through sex.

When I was fifteen I lost my virginity to a stranger at a party. He was tall and skinny with bleached hair. In my head he was 'Ace Face' in *Quadrophenia*. In reality he was just a fucked-up kid like me. We had terrible sex and, as I lay there on the cold tiles, legs spread, making the noises that I thought I was meant to make, I remember thinking, 'This is it?'

As we left the bathroom, he looked at his friends, laughed, and said, 'She hasn't got any tits.' I never saw him again.

Thirty-six years later I got breast cancer, twice, and had a double mastectomy. The irony was not lost on me.

I've been scarred for as long as I can remember. I carried my scars on the inside, and they burnt fierce and bright every day. They showed themselves through arrogance, through bulimia, through lack of self-care, of self-love. Years of twisted, burning pain, fuelled by biological family, appalling relationship choices and a desperate urge to get fucked and fuck up. This internal chaos created a fierce human with a determined will. An indestructible whirlwind that loved too hard, felt too much and wanted to experience everything. And for that, I am grateful.

Self-hatred, promiscuity and a desperate need to be loved by fucking anybody is a really shit place to reside as a human, but it's okay, because eventually, if you're really lucky – and fuck, I'm lucky – you find yourself, and cancer helped me do that. It did very strange things to me. It liberated me beyond belief.

It allowed me to live very much in the moment. To finally put myself first. It also brought me out of my shell, and gave me a confidence that I didn't know I had.

But initially, during diagnosis, that ridiculously harrowing time, when my entire sense of self turned once again upside-down and inside-out, the dancefloor became my place of salvation, my healing place. There I could lose myself. Switch off. Forget. Pretend for just one moment that it might not happen. That it was all a mistake.

I was surrounded by people telling me not to worry. That it was probably nothing. This didn't help. My go-to place, my safety net, had always been to expect the worst possible scenario. That way, I couldn't be let down, and anything else was a plus. My darling queerdos understood this when no one else did. They became my support network and kept me sane, and we spent hours, days, weeks, pulling apart sexuality, body image, life, death, and what it is to be human, travelling to all the dark corners of the psyche that most people would choose to avoid. The places where monsters lurk. Monsters like us.

During that time I was drawn back constantly to my teenage years, to where my obsession with long, lean, androgynous bodies came from: when I discovered queer.

I'd already decided to take not just the one but both breasts off and not reconstruct. I repeatedly refused the offer of prosthetics, pushing the giant bra back across the table to the breast nurse as she tried to convince me that I'd regret my decision. Fuck that. I wanted to be that body, but I was fucking terrified.

So I looked to Bowie for inspiration. My other hero. The man who fell to earth. Mutant. Freak. Glorious weirdo. I first became obsessed with him at seventeen. I was dating a 7-foot man who wore a full face of make-up and a floor-length trench coat, cinched tightly at the waist. His name was Rex and he hung out at beats, fucking men in the toilets. I thought it was the most romantic thing in the world.

I'd never quite been able to pin down my sexuality. I'd never felt the need to. I liked interesting people. At thirteen, tight blouses left me nervous and breathless, but so did the smell of pubescent boys who wanked too much. I was read as straight, but I mixed with an alternative crowd and the boys wore make-up and were prettier than most of us girls anyway. Rex was part of that crowd of fabulous misfits.

Rex loved Bowie. He had an enormous nose – my weakness, second only to the Madonna tooth gap – and copied Bowie's bright orange hair. My father hated him, completely threatened by his femininity and overtly camp nature. This made me gloriously happy.

Rex called me 'Vicki Wow', and painted my name on his bedroom wall in 2-foot-high letters, next to Bowie's and, sadly, next to the word heroin, which he spelt incorrectly. He wasn't too bright, but fuck, he was pretty. Rex lived with his parents, and his father was an ex-navy man. He'd camp it up for his mother and she'd look at me, horrified in her housecoat, and say, 'Ooh, Vicki, I don't know where he gets it from, his father's as straight as a die.' Straight out of a seventies British comedy.

Rex and I started hanging out at The Coven, Oxford's only gay club. It was favoured by punks and New Romantics, as it was the only interesting place in town. It had fake fibreglass rock cave booths and was tiny, and sleazy, and fabulous, and the bar was tended by a petite bottle blonde with a foul mouth and vicious wit. His name was Robert and he became our friend.

I worked in a cheese shop on Saturdays because I was still at school, and Robert and I quickly started up a convenient trade of cheddar for drinks. I'd hang out with him after school and he'd cook me soufflés and ratatouille. I truly felt I was living the most exotic life on the planet. I remember him mostly swanning around the flat wearing fluffy white towelling robes and mirror shades with a Duran Duran headband.

So we danced, and drank, and he continually tried to fuck my boyfriend and everything was soooo terribly glamorous in my tiny world.

To the soundtrack of Bowie I learnt to fuck, I learnt that gender was fluid, and I learnt that queer ran through me like a river.

So, life was good. I hung out with freaks and was finally free of judgement. But then shit went sideways, and suddenly sex, which had become fun and plentiful, and which I happily shared with many friends, became something I was judged for. I got in with a straighter crowd, got labelled a slut, and suddenly felt threatened in my hometown, so I fled and came to Sydney where I knew no one. I thought I could reinvent myself, but you never can. It all catches up with you in the end.

Here I was, a stranger in a new town, in the eighties. I took the plunge and bought an outfit that marked my official passing from backpacker to Sydneysider. Long socks, Dr. Martens shoes, a leotard top and enormous, baggy, wide-legged trousers from Zambesi, which I gathered and held up with a wide belt. It cost a fortune but I looked great. With my pale face and slash of bright red lipstick, hair slicked back, I looked like a mime. Perfectly androgynous.

I bought a ticket to the Biennale party. I'd never been to anything like it before. I took ecstasy and danced alone and then I made a friend. He was sweet and kind and we danced all night and then wandered through the Botanical Gardens while the sun rose over the harbour. His name was Brenton Heath-Kerr and he was my first friend in Sydney. Little was I to know the mark that gentle, unassuming soul would leave upon our queer landscape; that he would become one of Sydney's most brave and brilliant performance artists, who broke down stigma around HIV and turned his eventual death from AIDS into a performance piece. Brenton. Warrior. Visionary. Hero.

We lost touch when the rave scene hit Sydney. For a while there, shit got really straight before it bent right back to become what it is now. A delicious, queer, kooky mecca.

I was lucky to be hanging out with some serious freaks, one of whom, Lorna, turned up at my birthday party. Our partners were friends and I fell in love that day, a blistering, swooning love. I told a lesbian friend, begging for her help, not knowing if my crush was queer. It was Valentine's Day and I descended the stairs into the Oxford Street record store where Lorna worked, armed with a foil-covered chocolate heart, a gift for her. My friend was by my side ready to assess the sexuality of my new love. 'Straight,' she hissed in my ear. 'She's STRAIIIGHT.'

My 'straight' friend and I started an illicit love affair, sneaking up to Girl Bar at Kinselas to make out, leaving our boyfriends downstairs. We'd all go camping together and we'd find excuses to have alone time, and she'd leave bruises on the insides of my thighs with her teeth. I was smitten, but she tossed me aside with her gloriously vicious bad attitude. She's now my best friend, by my side forever. She was there as the surgeon broke the news of my diagnosis. She was there as they wheeled me into surgery. And she was the first thing I saw as I woke, breastless, from the anaesthetic. I love her to the end of the world and back.

So, when my old friends ask me 'What made you decide to be queer?' as if it was some magical moment, as if cancer made me gay, I tell them it's always been there. I never felt gay. I definitely didn't identify as a lesbian, and bi was way too restrictive. Queer fits me like a glove. It supports me; it moves with me. It winds its way through me and runs through my veins.

On occasion, I get hounded by my fellow queers for loving cock. Fuck that – I adore cock, be it hers, his or theirs. I adore pegging boys. These days, I fuck you because I want to. No one can tell me who to fuck, or who to love, or how to live. No one has the right to pass judgement or tell me I haven't fucked enough women to be queer. Queer is inside of me. It's the essence of me.

I love my logical family. I'd fucking die for them. I love my queer unofficially adopted son Jack, who tells me that his dick is bigger than mine, until I point out that I can just buy a bigger one. I love my queer boy fucks and my delicious girl-friends who kiss me forever. I love my straight tinder boy who asked, incredulous, 'What? You think we're not going to fuck anymore?' when I finally told him that they were cutting my tits off. Because yes, I did think that. I seriously thought that I'd never have sex again. But no, he called me a bad-assed bitch and fucked me against the wall before my scars had healed, and he still does, and I love him for that.

I didn't understand how anyone could love my nippleless, scarred torso, but they do, and most of all I do. To be freed from my stereotypically 'perfect' body after a lifetime of body image issues is an enormous relief, and to be liberated by the very thing I thought would kill me – having previously stated, 'I'd rather die than lose my breasts' – is beyond phenomenal.

I tear down people who say, 'You're still hot.'

'STILL.'

Fuck that shit.

I love my body.

I love my scars.

And I love every queer, fucked-up inch of me.

So queer comes in many guises and no one has the right to put parameters on that. No one has the deeds to queer. No one has to tick boxes x, y and z in order to qualify. To pass judgement on others as not fitting into the box of queer is to exclude and vilify.

We are smarter, stronger and infinitely more fabulous than those who try to take us down. We have fought more battles along the way than the average human will fight in a lifetime.

Being queer saved my life.

Thanks, Poly. Thanks, Bowie. Thank you.

Vicki Melson

Vicki Melson is a Sydney based aromatherapist with a background in graphic design. She has recently completed an Arts degree majoring in English and Film which she hopes will encourage her to write more. She escaped from the UK in 1987 and has since been trapped in Australia due to her love of its flora and fauna.

Vicki is a self-professed weirdo who overthinks everything, loves too hard, and likes cheese. She favours the flawed over the perfect, regularly obsesses over the life cycles of cicadas, and is scared of needles but not of death. She is a huge fan of the Oxford comma, and her safe word is orange.

MY MAN AND ME
Tim Bishop

My man and me, we travelled a lot, we got around. The first time I met him I knew I was in for something big, just from the look of it, and I was.

Early days and we were sitting in a pub at the back of Newtown, straight pub, and I said something across the corner of the bar that made him laugh, and he turns to me, that big cheesy smile half lifting him towards me and says, 'You know I could grow old with you, I could really grow old with you.'

In the days before he died, I reminded him of these words that had stuck so strongly in my mind. I told him I thought that over the years we had grown old together but he laughed, 'God, is that what I've done to you?' The truth was we had come that far. Just like an old married couple, we'd travelled on from the falling in love, made ourselves a family and stayed together, simply because we liked our lives this way, together.

We were equals and we lived in balance with one another. Oh I know I was the old woman but I liked that because it meant that he was my old man.

There was fear, that as quickly as I might let him into my life and heart, he'd be gone. He had a habit of whizzing through people's lives. I feared that every step deeper would be every step harder to then stand alone. The future was to be unknown and that's all that feeds fear, the unknown. See it, admit it but don't let it stop you.

He took me home the first summer, to his people. He was from Cabbage Tree Island on the Richmond River; I was from Albury on the Murray. North and south, top and bottom. He was salt water, I was fresh. He was from the warm, I was from the cold, but the biggest difference was that he knew his land as his people's, not just where he grew up but also the land of his People since time. That land was part of who he was, part of his pride, a proud man of the Bundjalung Nation. To know him and for us to really be a couple I had to know his land and his People. They're all inseparable.

There was plenty for me to fear going into this community but I wasn't afraid. He threw me in and I had to stand on my own two feet. But I was welcomed and cared for and respected as the person that their son and brother had brought home as his partner, and now he'd have to honour their acceptance of me. Besides. I hadn't broken any law, I came from the South, couldn't be related. The fact of my sex seemed to be overlooked and I relished in my new role of daughter-in-law. I got to hear all the goss. And they were the best times.

Before we'd leave, he'd pack the car with what he thought we'd need and I never knew what we had until we got there. All I had to do was pack my own clothes and it took as long for me to choose as it did for him to clean and pack the car and tidy the house ready for our return. He got this from his mother, just like the way he'd spread the sheets when he made the bed, like he was swimming across it.

He'd mostly drive and it'd take us about twelve hours to get there. We had our dream car, a 1964 Holden EH station wagon, bench seats. Thankfully, in spite of his lead foot, it didn't go very fast, so I'd relax. And we'd stop here and there and out'd come the matching picnic set, the camera, the radio and a blanket for my knees and we'd have tea and cakes on the tailgate. And we'd be off again, 'C'mon Nanna!' Music, black music, joints, sex on the road, relatives to drop shoes off to. I'd just lay back and go with it all.

His family, by now, were living off the island, in homes spread through the bush and amongst the cane fields. His mum, she'd had eleven kids. We'd camp down the back of hers and Lewis's, our own place, a place still called 'where Mark and Tim'd camp', 'cause we kept coming back. And there, under them big kookaburra trees, with the moon rising up over the river, you'd hear the night; it'd bring you things and you felt blessed. And there'd be kids for days, laughing and silly business, fights and tempers, music and parties, but most of all there'd be time. Time to sit and yarn with one another. You could relax. You'd hear stories and you'd learn.

He died in Sydney at our place.

We'd been camped in the hospital for about six weeks and it hadn't done much good. We decided together to go home and we had three days totally alone. We were ourselves again and we had the chance to be intimate, to be lovers. We were home.

The day before leaving the hospital for the last time, we'd gone home just for the afternoon to try things out. They wanted us to see if we thought that we could both manage. When we drove back to the hospital that evening, for the very last time, a big black bird swooped down and hovered over our bonnet. It's wingspan across our windscreen, leading our way to the end of the street. We both said nothin'. And I seen that bird come and go from around the house over the next three days.

And it happened. That moment that I'd feared the most, when I'd be lying with him but he'd be gone.

In the early light of that day, I rang to tell his dad and there was this big and brightly coloured bird through our window. One that I had never seen before.

We left in a Ford pick-up, farewelled Newtown and crossed the bridge, heading North, going home. I packed the picnic set for company but I didn't feel the excitement.

We drove that line that he had gone all his life, up and down, between the two places that drew him. And we stopped at the same stops, had tea and cakes and we passed 'em all on the way – Purfleet, Taree, Greenhill, Kempsey, 'Bucca, Yamba – and all in between to his own mob at Cabbo.

The driver, a blackfella, was a married man. He showed his respect for us and cared, knowing the honour of taking a brother home. We yarned a lot, talked like men and I told him about the best man that I had known, all the while him laying up over the back, listening and being with us. The driver showed his own pain, we'd reminded him of it. He'd lost his best mate some time back and hadn't thought about him for a while till now. And there really wasn't all that much difference.

For the first time, I'd be back there on my own. What would be their reaction to me? Would I cope? But I'd been shown how to stand on my own two feet and there was only warm love and respect for what had been endured. That night we had a big party around the fire, all of us together.

I still do go to them and they still come to me, 'cause we're family.

Tim Bishop

Tim Bishop is from Albury on the mighty Murray River, known as 'Indi' to the upper river First Peoples. Raised around open fires and kitchen tables, he is a singer-songwriter, storyteller and radio broadcaster, among other skills.

Tim has worked professionally as an actor, vocal and voice artist, an arts administrator, a theatre and costume designer, stage manager, tour manager and lighting designer and technician. He was co-producer of the Yabun Aboriginal and Torres Strait Islander Cultural Festival (2007–09) and was a founding team member of Gadigal Information Services, Koori Radio. He has also worked at the Redfern Community Centre as a teacher and mentor, in the centre's Studio Program.

You can read his work at **timbishop.com.au**.

MY MOTHERS TOLD ME STORIES

Maeve Marsden

My mothers told me stories in the filtered London light of our lounge room, in our brightly wallpapered kitchen, in their tiny bedroom, in that gentle way most parents do: 'First I must get the baby to sleep, and then make some dinner but after that I will play with you.' Three part narrative structures that helped me understand the tiny world I inhabited. Teresa, my British mother, told me her stories of growing up in working class Essex; from Louise came stories of her family's raucous pub in Catholic Campbelltown. And we knew the stories of their friends, too – warm, funny, strong-willed women who were so quick to laughter I thought that all the laughter in the world was within my reach.

The walls of our home were covered in bookshelves teeming with Sadako and her paper cranes, *Patience and Sarah*, *Playing Beatie Bow* and *Looking for Alibrandi*, the *Ramona* stories and

The Worst Witch, and *Bread and Jam for Frances*, a beloved childhood book about a charmingly strong-willed raccoon. All lovingly dewey-decimaled by librarian Teresa, as though this library of books and the echoing laughter of clever women could fortify us all against the world. Stories as armour.

We left London in 1988. That same year Prime Minister Margaret Thatcher introduced a bill to ensure local authorities did not 'promote the teaching in any maintained school of the acceptability of homosexuality as a pretended family relationship' – but this wasn't something I knew about at the time, and it could hardly have been my mothers' motivation for leaving considering queer families weren't offered a much warmer welcome down under.

We arrived in Australia to a country grappling with the bicentenary of invasion and colonisation, a country where my family – three kids born to two women – was not recognised, and where Teresa was forbidden from working. Partner visas for lesbian couples weren't an option, so Teresa spent her days cleaning houses for cash, and looking after me and my siblings – teaching us, playing with us, reading to us. When Louise arrived home from long shifts at the pharmacy, she would climb into my bed exhausted and, still in her white coat uniform, she would read to me, often falling asleep mid-chapter, glasses perched on the end of her nose, snoring gently.

My mothers read to me for comfort when I was small, and of course to help me learn to read, but as I grew we read more adult books together, discussing plot and character, discovering new worlds. I still love the books and music they shared with me throughout my childhood, but it wasn't these fictional tales that grew to form the basis of my identity. It was *our* stories, the story of my family, told over and over by my mothers, in so many ways and so many words, in so many places I couldn't tell you one instance when this storytelling took place.

Other families' histories are mapped out in genetics, in blood-lines. For other kids, the connection of shared blood holds such weight that a deep sense of belonging is contained in a simple, 'Oh, she has her father's smile.' Or her mother's eyes, her aunt's chin, her grandpa's nose. We examine babies for evidence. We joke, 'She's definitely yours,' or, 'Maybe the postman paid a visit.' This sense of belonging through DNA feels so natural and inevitable to most people that even now queer couples embarking on parenthood ask me with fear in their eyes whether I loved my parents equally, whether I ever felt lost, or like I didn't belong.

In our family we didn't have the unquestioned security of blood. My mothers mapped out our connections in every retelling of their love for me. When I was small they told me the story of how we were made in blunt and clear terms, easy for a child to digest. They told us so many times that I don't remember the not-knowing, I only remember from when I could already tell it myself.

Now that I am grown, I tell the story of my family with the benefit of hindsight and perspective, weaving in my politics, my adult sense of humour, a little sarcasm if I want to disarm the questioner. I have my own queer politics now, built through fierce debate with friends, lovers and yes, my family. But I will tell you my story as I told it when I was small, with simplicity and honesty, told so many times, to friends, teachers and curious strangers.

'I was born to two mothers, Louise and Teresa, in 1983 in West Hammersmith Hospital, London.'

'Which one's your real mum?'

'They both are . . .'

I always knew what they were asking, but I would still leave an awkward pause before giving them what they wanted. 'You know what I mean,' they'd say, and then either explicitly ask who gave birth or stare at me, imploring me not to make them say it.

'Teresa had Rowan. Then Louise had Gráinne and me. Rowan and Gráinne's donor is Graham. My donor is Dave, a New York Jew who lived in the same housing co-op as them in London. Louise and Dave were born on the same day, January 8th, Elvis's birthday. They used to run the finances at the co-op and everyone would steer clear when they were working because things got a little noisy. Genetically, my family makes a big W, well, a big zig-zag if you draw us out.'

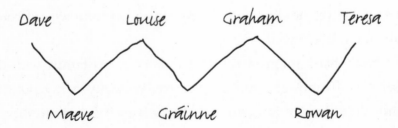

I drew that jagged line so many times, sometimes in the air, sometimes on paper. I drew it because I knew that's what people wanted of me. They wanted to know who shared blood with whom, whose sperm went in where. People are so horrified at the notion of children understanding sex and bodies, but their fears are quickly overwhelmed by morbid curiosity when faced with an eight year old who fully understands her own birds and bees.

'Dave's siblings didn't have kids when my parents asked him to donate for me. He agreed because his parents had been refugees and he didn't want kids of his own, but he wanted the bloodline to continue . . . No, I'm not Jewish, he is. He's not my dad, he's my sperm donor.' I don't remember the first time I was told that sperm + egg = baby.

Louise would tell me how she held Rowan just after Teresa gave birth, took this small baby in her arms and walked him up and down the ward whispering, 'I'm not sure what I'm doing but we're in this together, you and me. We're going to make this work, we have a job to do. You're mine. I am your mother and I love you and no one is going to take that away from us.'

Louise also told tales of growing up in the pub in Campbelltown with all her brothers and sisters, and her mother, Tibby, who was a golfing champion, 'Ma played golf there,' a constant refrain on family roadtrips. The Marsdens were a sprawling Irish Catholic clan, many publicans by trade, known for their boisterous energy and pack mentality. Two of her six siblings were also gay, John and Jane, the intersection of family and community more present for us than it is for most.

Louise told me about how I grew inside her, and how, three and a half years later when my sister was due, her waters broke while she was making her famous home-made hot chips and I ran around the house gathering towels while my brother hid in the corner complaining of a headache.

From Louise, I inherited a wanderlust as she told me tales of backpacking round Norway with her best friend, the big ship they sailed on from Australia, travelling through Eastern Europe before the Wall came down. Louise told me how she met Teresa at a job interview for a women's shelter in London, Teresa asked her out and she replied 'What?! I hardly know you!' But soon she was writing a letter to her parents to tell them she had fallen in love with a woman. Her father wrote back to her, 'As parents we teach you how to brush your hair, and brush your teeth, and we teach you how to love. But it's not our job to teach you who to love.'

Considering they both came out in the 1970s, it's surprising that both Louise and Teresa's families were fairly supportive of their daughters' sexualities. But despite fears for my mothers' safety in a homophobic world, they were. Teresa's mother, a staunch and quick-witted woman nicknamed Nanny Bingo due to her skill in the game, responded with characteristic bluntness and the perspective gained through years living in a cruel and difficult marriage. As far as she was concerned, as long as Teresa's partners weren't hitting or hurting her, they were welcome in Nanny's home.

Teresa turned the pain of growing up under the pressures of poverty and domestic violence into dark comedy, imitating all the voices of the characters from her childhood in thick Essex accents, English songs as well, so that the stories had a life, full and real. The pranks she and her siblings would play on Nanny Bingo took centre stage: nailing her slippers to the floor, or spooling a cotton reel out the upstairs window to knock at the door, collapsing in giggles over and over when Nanny opened it to no one. 'Oi, you kids!'

She didn't shy away from the blunt truth of it all, though. Hide and seek, a story of how Nanny hid Teresa in the cupboard during her father's rages. How Nanny finally left my grand-father – a man I never met – when Teresa was eleven, moving them to Devon where Teresa supported her through the divorce as best she could.

Teresa told me how she shared a bed with her siblings and would stroke her older sister's earlobe for comfort as she fell asleep. A colleague of Teresa's said once that I had inherited my round earlobes from Teresa and that they were good luck. Teresa and I smiled knowingly at each other, not correcting her genetic misconception.

My parents took up space in the community, protecting us and ensuring a place for our family, marching into the school-grounds to confront ignorant teachers or quietly speaking to parents who didn't want us coming over to play with their kids. Louise got a licence so she could set off the fireworks at the annual Summer Hill Primary School fireworks night, her small frame encased in bright orange coveralls, racing across the field to light spinners, rockets, Catherine wheels, roman candles. Nearby, Teresa (wo)manned the vegie burger stand, her secret recipe growing ever more popular until, finally, when I was in year 6, victory was ours: we outsold the sausage sizzle.

I write the stories of my childhood here because I don't know how to make this book without them. In a book of stories shaped by identity, I don't know how to write about something else. I am thirty-four years old, I have travelled strange and wonderful places and loved strange and wonderful people; I've had more misadventures than adventures, hilarious, heartbreaking and true. But I come back to this queer family history time and again because I've been telling it so long it's become my heart. I feel it at the far reaches of my ribcage, in the pit of my stomach and in loud blood rushing, this family of mine.

When my parents split up in 2005 this story was disrupted, this tale I had told over and over till I grew into someone who spoke and spoke and had to be reminded to shut up. I was facing not only the pain of my family's separation but also the destruction of the public image and identity we had constructed. And I wasn't alone. Some of their lesbian friends were remarkably angry. 'What will we tell our kids?' they said. It seemed my family had become part of their story too, the example they held up when their fears took over and they wondered if this new way of parenting was okay. 'Look at Teresa and Louise, they've been together twenty-eight years. Look at their kids. Look how happy they are.'

The year after Teresa moved out of our family home, and I moved back from uni in regional NSW to live with Louise was the worst of my life. In this day and age most people's parents have split up at some point, so it seems like hyperbole, but I had held on to my family's unity to build myself up as a person. It was my identity and I had lost it.

Also, my mothers behaved like total dickheads. Teresa lied and cheated, and in the midst of her heartbroken breakdown, Louise lost sight of her boundaries as my mother, told me too much and added to the strain on my relationship with Teresa. When I tell my story, I usually leave this part out, 'the divorce'. I don't tell people how we yelled and raged, how my mothers fought over money for two years, that I only found out how long it took because my ex-girlfriend, then a court reporter, saw them in court with their lawyers. I don't tell people that in 2006, my first year of work, fresh out of uni and ready to take on the world, Louise would climb into my bed each morning and sob and sob and sob, grieving not only her relationship but also her oldest brother, John, who died that same year. I would get into my little car to drive to work, playing the same song on repeat over and over and over while I sobbed and sobbed as well. With all the crying I did in cars that year, not to mention the crying Louise sometimes did while I was in the passenger seat, it's a wonder we never crashed. I haven't told anyone, I don't think, that when I couldn't sleep I pictured walking into Teresa's apartment, marching silently to her kitchen then taking the plates out of the cupboard one by one and smashing them: I've always had a fairly obvious grasp of metaphor.

I leave these stories out because they aren't the ones my community wants to hear. They don't fit the Love-is-Love narrative we've been selling to Australia for over a decade. People want to watch the adorable grannies, together for fifty years, finally getting hitched; they want the little boy desperate to be a ring bearer, or indeed flower girl, at his dads' wedding; they want to hear about how happy our childhood was, not how it all fell apart. My siblings and I were living in three different cities the year my parents split us and I still see us in my mind's eye, sitting alone in Sydney, Bathurst and Canberra, not quite able to unite against our parents as they self-destructed. We fell so hard and fast from the pedestal I had placed us on.

When I don't tell these stories I do us a disservice. Stories aren't press releases for a cause. We should have never been poster children, a position we held through no fault of our own, or our parents', but because broader society didn't understand us, and were scared, inexplicably, of a family without a mum and a dad and a nice, neat family tree. We performed our successes for others because we were afraid that if we weren't perfect, people would blame my mothers' lesbianism. But we were all just flawed little people, and stories have conflict and drama and pain. And sometimes, resolution.

If we hadn't hurt so much, it wouldn't have meant so much when my mothers started to reach out to each other in friendship. Now, thirteen years later, we can all sit around a dinner table for birthdays. They come to the airport together to farewell me on my longer trips, they catch up for coffee every now and then, and they go to the opera together on occasion because everyone in our family has a passion for melodrama. No friendship or relationship is perfect, but my parents loved us kids so hard that they weren't willing to leave things unresolved; they rebuilt our family in a new way and started a new chapter. And, thanks to all the lesbian emotional processing we did during the fall out (some stereotypes hold kernels of truth), my understanding of adult relationships has progressed past what I knew at twenty-two. Their break-up wasn't the soap opera drama of infidelity I saw at the time, a simplistic explanation which hides the complexity of years; it was another step in the most complicated of dances between two women over monogamy, sexuality, class, gender, pregnancy, birth, raising children, migration, intimacy with friends, family obligation, work, money, growing up and growing older.

And so, my story is one about stories. It is a story of queer culture and family, and of finding my place in the world. I see my life in chapters and I share it that way too. 'Have I told you the saga of my French ex-girlfriend?' I'll say, before launching in, performing my life for people in little vignettes, tidbits of romance, adventure, comical failure. 'What about the time I was involved in the largest land rescue in Australian history? Well, largest at the time . . . twenty-three theatre students airlifted out of the blue mountains.'

Perhaps this sense of self-importance – this notion that I am living out my own coming-of-age drama at every turn – came from always being someone people noticed. I was memorable, not necessarily because of my personality or even my rather uncommon name, but because of my differences. My story marked me as 'the kid with two mums' and the more people remembered me, the more I expected them to. I am unquestionably, unapologetically, an attention-seeker, and I have turned that quality into a career.

As I write this, I am in a new chapter with my love – a woman who reminds me, sometimes, of my lesbian aunts and my mothers' friends, those queer women I grew up among: smart, resilient, honest, funny, ready to take on the world. In the quiet cocoon of our bedroom, we tell each other stories late into the night and, hopefully, one day soon, there'll be little humans in our home who we can read to, who will look up at our shelves of books, at our walls covered in photos, and make their own histories too.

I have beautiful, grand, wide-eyed hope for our life together but I also know that stories, especially personal stories, never get tied up in a neat bow shimmering with domesticity and happiness. As a lesbian, as a queer woman and as a feminist, I will not put all my eggs in the basket of a relationship, even one this lovely. I seek community, and I try to help build community, because like my mothers I know it is the lifeblood for the marginalised. Because queer family isn't about the physical or the biological, it's about that intangible *something* that we find in others when we have found ourselves.

Maeve Marsden

Maeve Marsden is a writer, director, producer and performer. Her writing has appeared in the *Sydney Morning Herald, Guardian Australia*, Junkee, SBS Online, ArtsHub and Daily Review, and she recently edited the ABC's Sydney Mardi Gras 40th Anniversary Magazine. Maeve produces, directs and performs in comedy, cabaret, live music and storytelling, enjoying critically acclaimed seasons at Sydney Festival, the Sydney Opera House, Adelaide Cabaret Festival, Melbourne International Comedy Festival and Edinburgh Festival Fringe, among others. As a child of same-sex parents, Maeve is passionate about the rights of diverse families, and she writes and speaks on the issue often, appearing in ABC2 documentary *Growing Up Gayby* and consulting on feature documentary, *Gayby Baby*. Maeve likes gin, dancing, cheese and TV melodramas with good ethics and bad dialogue.

She tweets from **@maevemarsden**.

ACKNOWLEDGEMENTS

First and most importantly, thanks to the writers who have contributed their stories, thoughts, ideas, passion, humour and hearts to Queerstories, not only in this book but on stage at the events. Along with the incredible Queerstories audience, you have helped build a community, a supportive space for queer storytelling that celebrates LGBTQIA+ narratives and creativity.

Thank you to the City of Sydney, first for allowing me to test the Queerstories concept at Late Night Library in 2015, then for the funding support in 2017 through the Arts and Cultural Grant program; to Giant Dwarf in Sydney, for being the kind of venue that centres artists and truly wants to collaborate, and to my wonderful interstate venues, Howler in Melbourne and Brisbane Powerhouse. Special mention to those who have contributed so much to the Queerstories events in Sydney: Ali Graham, Nikita Agzarian, David Harmon, Fran Middleton,

Alana Shootingstar, photographer Patrick Boland, and, of course, Neil Phipps, Amanda Galea and Natalie Kull – Auslan interpreters to the stars.

Thank you to my publisher Robert Watkins and my editor Brigid Mullane, as well as Kate Stevens, Andy Palmer, and the rest of the team at Hachette Australia.

Finally to my family, chosen and otherwise, who give me unending love and who – through their humour, intellect, creativity and support – have allowed me to live happily and pursue a career as an independent artist and producer: my parents, Teresa Savage and Louise Marsden; my partner Nikki Stevens and our perfect dog Frank; my businesswife Phoebe Meredith; my lesbian aunts (too many to name); and my other favourite people: Rowan Savage, Gráinne Marsden, Anna Martin, Amy Coopes, Nicola Gleeson Coopes, Viv McGregor, Jane Marsden, Joy Marshall, Sally Shrubb, Molly Tregoning, Penny Crofts, Ali Benton, Emily Falconer and Cameron Power.

hachette
AUSTRALIA

If you would like to find out more about Hachette Australia,
our authors, upcoming events and new releases you can visit
our website or our social media channels:

hachette.com.au

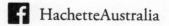 HachetteAustralia

 HachetteAus